BOUNCING BACK
After Your Pregnancy

DISCARD

D0815917

Other books by
Glade B. Curtis, M.D., and Judith Schuler, M.S.

Your Pregnancy Week by Week, 4th Edition

Your Pregnancy: Every Woman's Guide

Your Pregnancy After 35, Revised Edition

Your Pregnancy Questions and Answers, 3rd Edition

Your Baby's First Year Week by Week

BOUNCING BACK
After Your Pregnancy

What You Need to Know
about Recovering from
Labor and Delivery and
Caring for Your New Family

Glade B. Curtis, M.D.

Judith Schuler, M.S.

PERSEUS PUBLISHING

Cambridge, Massachusetts

Cataloging-in-Publication Data is available from the Library of Congress
ISBN 0-7382-0606-7

Perseus Publishing is a member of the Perseus Books Group
Visit us on the World Wide Web at http://www.perseusbooks.com

Perseus Publishing books are available at special discounts for bulk purchases in the U.S. by corporations, institutions, and other organizations. For more information, please contact the Special Markets Department at the Perseus Books Group, 11 Cambridge Center, Cambridge, MA 02142, or call (800) 255-1514 or (617)252-5298, or e-mail j.mccrary@perseusbooks.com.

Text design by Cynthia Young
Set in 11-point Berling Roman by The Perseus Books Group
Illustrations by Leslie Elfner and David Fischer

First printing, January 2002

1 2 3 4 5 6 7 8 9 10—03 02 01

CONTENTS

ACKNOWLEDGMENTS

There are many people to thank for their help and support during the preparation of this book. Without their understanding and assistance, it would have been a much more difficult task.

Glade B. Curtis—I want to thank my wife, Debbie, for her support. She's always there, in good times and hard times, ready and willing to help in any way she can. Thanks, too, to my five children, who try to be understanding of the time and effort a project like this requires. Without the love and support of my parents, I wouldn't be where I am today. Special thanks to Megan and Scott Harbertson for their computer expertise.

Judith Schuler—Thanks to my son, Ian, for your understanding and acceptance of all the time and travel I've had to put in on all of our books. And I greatly appreciate your love and support, Mom and Dad. Also, my deepest gratitude to Bob Rucinski for your help with so many other things, especially those involving the computer. I couldn't have made heads or tails of any of it without your assistance. Many thanks to Leslie Elfner for your help with this book.

THIS IS THE BEGINNING!

Participating in the birth of a baby is exciting for everyone in-volved—the new parents, family members and friends. It's also exciting for the medical personnel who have been privileged to care for you and your baby before birth. To those ends—the care of you and your unborn baby—we have written four other books dealing with pregnancy: *Your Pregnancy Week by Week; Your Pregnancy Questions and Answers; Your Pregnancy After 35* and *Your Pregnancy: Every Woman's Guide.* In addition, we have also written a book about baby's first year, *Your Baby's First Year Week by Week.*

This book covers the period following your baby's birth. Because this is also an important time in *your* life, the material we include is intended to help guide you through the many new experiences awaiting you. We even include information to help you plan future pregnancies. We hope the topics we have covered provide the information you need as you begin your new life as a parent.

Note: In referring to the baby, we have chosen to alternate the use of male and female pronouns in each chapter. In odd-numbered chapters, we refer to the baby with the pronouns "she" and "her"; in even-numbered chapters, we use "he" and "him."

SOS and *Fast Facts*—In each chapter, you will find boxes titled "SOS" and "Fast Facts." The SOS boxes alert you to situations in which you should "Seek Outside Help" (SOS), such as the occurrence of physical problems. The boxes of "Fast Facts" are snippets of information you may find interesting that add to your understanding of the postpartum period.

RECOVERY OVERVIEW

IN THE HOSPITAL

What Hurts:

- Everything! Sore muscles from the effort of childbirth and labor may be compared to the soreness felt after running a marathon.

- Your bottom is sore and swollen; if you had an episiotomy, it hurts.

- Your incision, if you had a C-section or tubal ligation, will be very tender.

What Works:

- You can finally hold your baby.

- The nurse call button—use it whenever necessary!

- You can sleep on your stomach again.

- Try different ways for you and your partner to bond with baby.

What Doesn't Work:

- Don't sit in one spot for very long.

- Feeding (breast or bottle) the new miracle in your arms is a little scary, but you'll get the hang of it.

- Your baby didn't come with instructions.

What Spells Trouble:

- Heavy bleeding or passing blood clots larger than an egg.

- High or low blood pressure.

- Pain unrelieved by medication.

- Fever over 101.5F (25.25C).

It's OK If:

- You cry or feel emotional.

- You rest. Ask to turn off your phone and to restrict visitors.

- You sigh with relief. You did it! You might even think or say, "That wasn't so bad."

Don't Look Now, But . . .

- You just lost 12 pounds—7 pounds of baby, 2 pounds of placenta, 3 pounds of blood and amniotic fluid. It'll take awhile for the rest of your weight to come off.

- You probably won't be wearing your fashionable jeans home from the hospital.

Remember to:

- Eat nutritiously to keep up energy and for milk production, if you breastfeed.

- Write down thoughts and feelings about labor, delivery and the first hours with your new baby. Encourage your partner to do the same.

- Watch hospital videos about baby care. Ask staff for clarification or help.

- Get the name, address and telephone number of your pediatrician.

Call in the Troops:

- Ask questions, and get help from the nurses and staff in the hospital.

- Ask your partner to take you for a walk outside your hospital room.

Stop and Smell the Roses:

- Take time for you, your partner and your baby to bond as a family. Was that a miracle or what?

Red Light, Green Light

Red Light—Don't overdo it. Keep phone conversations and visits manageable. Don't tire yourself out entertaining others.

Green Light—Splurge, and eat something you didn't eat during pregnancy.

1ST WEEK HOME

What Hurts:

- You'll have painful uterine contractions, especially during nursing.

- Your breasts are full of milk, engorged and leaking.

- The area of your episiotomy or tear is still sore. You won't want to go horseback riding soon!

What Works:

- You can move around a lot easier without carrying baby, placenta and amniotic fluid.

- Muscles are still sore.

- Maternity clothes may still be the most comfortable to wear.

What Doesn't Work:

- Your legs are still swollen.

- You leak urine or stool and can't control it.

What Spells Trouble:

- Bleeding gets heavier, or you pass blood clots.

- You get red streaks or hard spots in your breasts.

- You develop a fever.

It's OK If:

- You don't keep up with the housework.

- You cry, sigh or laugh for no reason.

- You ask for help from friends and family.

Don't Look Now, But . . .

- You look a little pregnant from the side.

- You still are carrying some of the extra weight you gained during pregnancy.

Remember to:

- Make baby's first appointment with the doctor.

- Have baby added to your insurance policy. There may be a time limit for this, so don't delay.

- Keep important "baby" documents together, such as the birth certificate, immunization record (when you get it at baby's first pediatrician's visit) and his social security card.

- Make your 6-week postpartum checkup appointment.

- Plan on making daycare arrangements, if you haven't started already.

Call in the Troops:

- Give your partner a job or assignment to help you and to make him feel useful.

- Contact La Leche League, if you are having any problems with breastfeeding.

Stop and Smell the Roses:

- Have you ever seen a cuter baby?

Red Light, Green Light

Red Light—Avoid exercise and sex. Don't use tampons to deal with *lochia* (bleeding).

Green Light—Do your Kegel exercises.

2ND WEEK HOME

What Hurts:

- Your breasts (whether or not you breastfeed) are still full and uncomfortable.

- Hemorrhoids still hurt, but they may be getting better.

What Works:

- With swelling and water retention diminishing, you can wear some of your shoes again.

- Feeding (by breast or bottle) is starting to work better; you are actually going to be able to do this!

What Doesn't Work:

- When you cough, laugh, sneeze or lift something heavy, you may lose stool or urine and not be able to control it.

- Fatigue! Taking care of baby requires a lot of time and energy.

What Spells Trouble:

- A foul odor or yellow-green vaginal discharge; lochia should be decreasing at this point.

It's OK If:

- You let baby cry a little before checking on her.

Don't Look Now, But . . .

- You can almost see your feet when you look down (your tummy is getting smaller).

Remember to:

- Write down any questions for your visit with your pediatrician.

- Keep your doctor's appointment to have your incision checked if you had a C-section.

Call in the Troops:

- Neighbors love to help with new babies. If you don't know them well, asking for their help with a new baby is a good icebreaker.

Stop and Smell the Roses:

- Is there anything softer than your baby's skin?

- Write down some of your thoughts and feelings in your journal.

Red Light, Green Light

Red Light—Hold off on any kind of exercise that puts a strain on your abdomen.

Green Light—Take a short walk outside.

3RD WEEK HOME

What Hurts:

- Swelling and soreness around your bottom are decreasing, but sitting for a long time doesn't feel very good.

What Works:

- Swelling in hands decreases. If you took off your rings during pregnancy, try them on again.

What Doesn't Work:

- Baby doesn't know the difference between night and day, so your sleep patterns are also disturbed.

- Getting ready to go anywhere is like planning a major trip. It takes three times longer to get ready with baby as it used to before baby.

- Your mother-in-law decided she could stay and help for another week. (Actually, this might be good.)

What Spells Trouble:

- Red streaks or tender, hard spots on your legs, particularly the backs of your calves. This could signify a blood clot.

It's OK If:

- You feel sad or depressed some of the time. You may even cry.

- You miss being pregnant. (Just don't tell anyone!)

Don't Look Now, But . . .

- You've got varicose veins, just like your mother! They'll get better as you recover from pregnancy and begin exercising again.

- The skin on your abdomen still looks stretched out when you stand up.

Remember to:

- Keep baby's first appointment with the pediatrician. You'll probably receive his immunization record at this visit. Put it in a safe place with baby's other important papers.

- Talk to friends who can relate to your experience.

- Take lots of pictures and videos! You'll be amazed how quickly baby will change as he grows.

Call in the Troops:

- Keep your partner involved. Let him try his hand at caring for baby. And ask for his help with household chores.

Stop and Smell the Roses:

- By now you've changed over 200 diapers; you're an expert.

Red Light, Green Light

Red Light—No douching. Follow instructions you got in the hospital for taking care of your episiotomy.

Green Light—It's OK to talk to your partner about baby blues. Let him help.

4TH WEEK HOME

What Hurts:

- Muscles feel better, and you can do more now. Be aware—it's easy to pull or to strain muscles you haven't used for a while.

What Works:

- Control of urine and stool are improving. Doing your Kegel exercises is paying off.

- Baby is showing signs of adjusting to a regular schedule.

What Doesn't Work:

- Things that once were easy to do, such as bending over or lifting, may be harder now. Take things slowly, and allow yourself plenty of time for even the easiest chores.

- Your first menstrual period after delivery could happen at any time. If you don't breastfeed, your first period is usually 4 to 9 weeks after delivery, but it can happen earlier.

What Spells Trouble:

- Blood in your urine, dark or cloudy urine or severe cramping or pain with urination—all are symptoms of a urinary-tract infection (UTI).

It's OK If:

- You leave baby with a friend or relative while you do something for yourself, such as exercise, go shopping or have lunch with a friend.

Don't Look Now, But . . .

- You've been walking and doing light exercise, and it feels OK, but the weight isn't disappearing as quickly as you'd like it to.

Remember to:

- Check on your 6-week appointment with your doctor. Write down questions you have as they come to you.

Call in the Troops:

- A night out with your partner is a good plan. Grandparents or friends can babysit, if you ask them.

Stop and Smell the Roses:

- The time you have with your new baby is precious. Soon you may be going back to work or returning to other activities. You may not believe it now, but a baby grows up faster than you think.

Red Light, Green Light

Red Light—Avoid high-impact exercises, hard sit-ups or lifting weights.

Green Light—Walking is good; gradually increase distance and time. Find another new mom and together walk the babies in their strollers.

5TH WEEK HOME

What Hurts:

- Very little compared to 5 weeks ago!

- As you get back to regular activities, sore muscles and a sore back may be expected.

What Works:

- Bowel movements may still be sore in the area of your episiotomy or your rectum from time to time.

- Bladder and bowel control have returned.

- You may be getting a little anxious to go back to work. You have missed your friends and the work you do.

What Doesn't Work:

- You—but you may be returning to work soon.

- It may be hard to go back to work and not be there for every moment with your baby.

What Spells Trouble:

- Not planning for after-birth contraception. Decide on some type of birth control and be ready to start it.

- Feeling depressed, blue or sad every day. Baby blues should be getting much better, if they haven't disappeared already.

It's OK If:

- You're a little nervous about going back to work. You may even have a touch of baby blues occasionally.

Don't Look Now, But . . .

- Clothes may still be a little snug.

- When you go in for your 6-week postpartum checkup, you'll have to get weighed again.

- You meet a friend you don't see often, and she asks you when your baby is due.

Remember to:

- Remind yourself it took 9 months of pregnancy to gain the weight you did and it'll take awhile to get back your prepregnancy figure.

Call in the Troops:

- Returning to work requires planning. Start now to put your "back-to-work" schedule into effect.

- Plans for daycare, tending, nursing and other things need to be in place soon. Family and friends can be an important ingredient.

Stop and Smell the Roses:

- Have you noticed the smile on your partner's face? How proud he is when he holds the baby and talks about him.

Red Light, Green Light

Red Light—Still red for sex and heavy exercise, but you're getting closer to the Green Light.

Green Light—Do a little more exercise, such as swimming and walking, if you have stopped bleeding and are doing well.

6TH WEEK HOME

What Hurts:

- Having a pelvic exam at your 6-week checkup isn't usually as bad as you might expect. Your episiotomy has probably healed by now, so this won't be much of a discomfort.

What Works:

- In the space of 6 weeks, your uterus has gone from the size of a watermelon to the size of your fist; it now weighs only about 2 ounces.

- Your visit with your doctor may be one of the more enjoyable ones. Think of all the women in the waiting room; some are just getting started.

What Doesn't Work:

- Forgetting to keep or not making your 6-week postpartum appointment. It's important. Plan to discuss several important subjects, such as contraception, your current activity level, limitations and future pregnancies. (Be sure to discuss postpartum depression if you are still having problems.)

- The little sign in the office window that says, "Doctor is in delivery." You now understand a lot better about what happens in delivery and how much you wanted your doctor there with you.

What Spells Trouble:

- Baby blues or feeling depressed every day.

- Vaginal bleeding or a foul-smelling discharge.

- Pain or swelling in your legs.

- Red or tender breasts.

It's OK If:

- You're happy not to be pregnant.

- You wish you were still pregnant.

Don't Look Now, But . . .

- When you get weighed at the office, you weigh the same or more than at your first OB visit.

Remember to:

- Ask questions; make a list. Good questions include: What are my choices for contraception? Do I have any limitations as far as exercise or sex? Is there anything I should know from this pregnancy and delivery if I decide to get pregnant again?

- If you take baby with you, take plenty of supplies. You may have to wait.

- If you're going back to work soon, check on childcare arrangements.

Call in the Troops:

- There are still times when you need help. Continue to involve your partner as much as possible.

- People in your doctor's office have probably been helpful to you. Thank them for their help, and ask if you can call with future questions.

Stop and Smell the Roses:

- You did it! Pat yourself and your partner on the back.

- Continue to write down thoughts and feelings in your journal. Encourage your partner to do the same.

> ### Red Light, Green Light
>
> **Red Light**—If you talk with women in the waiting room at your doctor's office, don't scare them with the hardest parts of pregnancy and labor and delivery from your own experiences.
>
> **Green Light**—Exercise and sex, or sex and exercise (or sex as exercise!).

3 MONTHS

What Hurts:

- You may have sore muscles from exercising—a little more than a month ago, you were given the OK to do any exercises you wanted.

What Works:

- You probably have had your first period by now if you are bottlefeeding.

What Doesn't Work:

- Your first period could be heavier, longer and different from those before pregnancy.

What Spells Trouble:

- You haven't done anything about contraception, unless you want to celebrate two birthdays in the same year.

It's OK If:

- You let baby cry when she's a little fussy and needs to soothe herself.

Don't Look Now, But . . .

- The pounds and inches aren't disappearing as quickly as you would like.

Remember to:

- Write down baby's milestones as they happen; write them in baby's book or keep a journal.

Call in the Troops:

- Look for things your partner can do to be involved in baby's care. Let him help out when he can.

- If you've stopped breastfeeding, let baby's dad give her a bottle.

Stop and Smell the Roses:

- About a year ago, you were just learning you were pregnant. Look how well you did!

Red Light, Green Light

Red Light—Be careful about not using contraception or considering another pregnancy this soon.

Green Light—Increase your exercise schedule.

6 MONTHS

What Hurts:

- Getting on the scale. But hang in there, and keep working hard on good nutrition and exercise!

What Works:

- Your first period, if you are breastfeeding.

- Your family and friends are eager to help out.

What Doesn't Work:

- Your first period, if you are breastfeeding. It could be heavier, longer and different from those before pregnancy.

- Don't try to do it all yourself. Let your partner and others help.

What Spells Trouble:

- You are still feeding baby every 2 or 3 hours. A feeding schedule should be established by now.

It's OK If:

- You take time for yourself. Arrange time for regular activities, such as exercising, baby play groups and meeting with other new moms.

Don't Look Now, But . . .

- You're starting to fit into some of your clothing from before pregnancy.

Remember to:

- Share special baby moments with your partner.

- Record baby's noises, or take pictures. A tape recorder or video camera are great for this!

Call in the Troops:

- Find a friend with a baby, and trade childcare duties. It's a good way for each of you to find time for yourself.

Stop and Smell the Roses:

- Things are falling into place and working out.

Red Light, Green Light

Red Light—Be careful about expecting too much from your baby, such as walking or talking early. Enjoy baby for who he is now. Accomplishments will come soon.

Green Light—Find picture books and toys that you and baby can enjoy together.

---

1 YEAR

What Hurts:

- Breastfeeding, if baby has teeth!

What Works:

- All systems are go! It's taken time, energy and hard work, but your life is going smoothly now.

- Baby is on schedule and sleeps through the night most of the time.

What Doesn't Work:

- Baby's schedule is probably not perfect all the time!

What Spells Trouble:

- Tending to baby's care but ignoring your own.

- Missing your yearly exam and Pap smear.

It's OK If:

- You are considering another pregnancy.

Don't Look Now, But . . .

- Your body is returning to its prepregnancy shape. Your tummy is flat, you've lost most of the pregnancy weight and you feel great.

Remember to:

- Continue taking care of yourself. Eat nutritiously, get enough rest and continue exercising.

- Write down feelings about this time in your life. Encourage your partner to do the same.

Call in the Troops:

- Sharing childcare can be a good way to develop baby play groups. Interacting with other children is good for baby.

Stop and Smell the Roses:

- Baby's 1st birthday is just around the corner. Celebrate!

- Enjoy baby's first words, first steps and every other "first" that will happen.

- Continue taking pictures of baby.

Red Light, Green Light

Red Light—Don't compare yourself to any other women who have a child the same age. You're all different, and so are your babies! Every baby reaches milestones at the right age for him or her.

Green Light—If you're considering another pregnancy soon, think about all the things you want to do before you get pregnant, such as getting your weight under control, discussing medication use with your doctor and addressing other health issues.

1

Your Pregnancy Is Over!

The end of labor, and the birth of your baby, is a wonderful beginning. Your beautiful baby has arrived, and you and your partner are filled with joy, love and happiness that you are now a family. You are busy enjoying your new baby and the attention of family and friends. You are probably anxious to get on with the role of parenting.

The first 6 weeks immediately after your baby's birth, called the *postpartum period*, involve great adjustment. You may have many questions about this time, such as those listed below.

- How long will it take me to feel normal again?
- What are the different ways to feed my baby?
- How can I get my body back in shape?
- How can I take care of my baby and not neglect my partner?
- Should I return to work?
- How can we find a caregiver?

All these questions and concerns, and many others, are addressed in this book. You may choose to read all the information here, or you may want to check out the sections or chapters that are of most interest to you right now.

....

FAST FACTS

Many women express surprise at how physically tired they feel after labor and delivery. They often remark how sore all their muscles are. If you feel this way, it's the result of the hard physical work you did during labor and delivery.

....

CHANGES IN YOU

Your body undergoes major changes as you begin to recover from pregnancy, labor and delivery. You'll go through physical and emotional adjustments, but this doesn't mean you're ill. Take good care of yourself to get back in shape—physically and mentally—to face the challenges ahead. Let others help you.

The time you spend in the hospital after delivery can be very helpful to you—so take advantage of it. You can learn ways to deal with the many things happening to you. Most hospitals or delivery suites have educational channels or videotapes on various subjects, such as breastfeeding and childcare, that you can watch while you're there. Learn as much as you can about what is normal after delivery. Ask questions, and follow the advice of your doctors and nurses.

. . . .

FAST FACTS

During pregnancy, your body stored up to 10 pounds (4.5kg) of fat to provide you energy for the first few months after your baby's birth.

. . . .

IMMEDIATELY FOLLOWING BIRTH

Immediately after birth, your uterus begins shrinking rapidly, which helps control bleeding. The uterus is also returning to its normal prepregnancy state. As hormone levels become normal, you may feel emotional.

You may be a little woozy the first few times you get out of bed. Your body may feel stiff and sore from the delivery. Your back may ache. Your body may retain fluid. You may find yourself perspiring more. If you had an *episiotomy*, a controlled cut made by your doctor during delivery, the area may be sore or tender. If you had a Cesarean delivery, your abdomen may be sore, and you may not be able to get around very quickly.

The good news is that these are all temporary conditions! Soon you'll have more energy and feel better, and each of these changes will be a memory.

. . . .

FAST FACTS

Stretch marks don't just occur on the abdomen; they can be found on the breasts, legs, buttocks and arms.

. . . .

SOME CHANGES YOU MAY EXPERIENCE

After your baby's birth, you will have a discharge of blood, called *lochia*. This bleeding occurs with both vaginal and Cesarean deliveries, although it may not be quite as heavy with a C-section.

You may have some pain in the perineum—the area between the vagina and the rectum—caused by stretching, tearing or cutting the area to allow for delivery of the baby. The pain from your episiotomy may be fairly uncomfortable, but it heals quickly.

Contractions of your uterus may occur for several days after your baby is born. These signal that the uterus is shrinking to its prepregnancy size (or as close as it will come to it). You may notice the same discomfort when you breastfeed because breastfeeding causes the uterus to contract.

Your breasts may feel sore or tender, whether you breastfeed or bottlefeed. You can't stop the natural process of breast milk coming in, even if you do not plan to nurse your baby.

You may be surprised how hungry you are after your baby's birth. Reward yourself! Order something that will make you feel special. Have your partner bring special food into the hospital, or have a meal catered for both of you. A word of caution—if you're breastfeeding, avoid chocolate. It could pass into your milk and upset baby's tummy.

S O S

Your bleeding should steadily decrease. If you experience an increase, such as from one to two pads a day to one to two pads an hour, call your doctor immediately.

Exercise can help you feel better faster. Begin doing very light exercises, such as stretching your muscles, while you're still in the hospital. Walking is good exercise. You will probably be advised to be careful with your activity if you had a Cesarean delivery; avoid activities that may strain your abdominal muscles.

SOS

 Call your doctor if your breasts become hard, if they have red streaks or if you develop a high fever. These are signs of a breast infection.

OTHER CONDITIONS YOU MAY EXPERIENCE

Constipation, uncomfortable bowel movements and hemorrhoids may be other results of pregnancy. Delivery can slow the movement of food through the intestines, which may cause you to feel bloated or constipated. Taking pain medicine, making changes in your diet and spending more time in bed may cause changes in your bowel function. Drink plenty of fluids, eat bran and prunes, and take stool softeners to help with the problem.

....

FAST FACTS

Hormone changes during pregnancy can stimulate hair growth; your hair may seem thicker and healthier. After delivery, you may notice an increase in hair loss. You are *not* going bald! Hair growth will return to its normal pattern within a few months after delivery.

....

You may experience incontinence (reduced ability to control your flow of urine) for a short period. As bladder muscles contract and grow stronger, it will pass.

You may be emotional at times after the birth of your baby. Mood swings are usually mild, but some women experience more severe feelings of sadness. Other emotions are also common. Feelings you may experience include elation, feelings of inadequacy and feeling overwhelmed by your new responsibilities. For more information about these emotional changes, see Chapter 3, page 45.

···

FAST FACTS

You may feel a range of emotions after baby's birth. You may even feel "out of the limelight" because you're no longer the center of attention. All these feelings are normal.

···

BONDING WITH YOUR BABY

Have you heard how important it is to "bond with your baby"? What is bonding? Is it really important in your life with baby? When does it happen? How does it happen?

Bonding is a process that usually takes longer than one instance for it to occur. It's the process of becoming emotionally attached to your child, and it deepens over time.

Bonding occurs between each parent and his or her child. We once believed bonding was purely an emotional response; today researchers believe there is a physical aspect to bonding. You can bond with your baby the first time in the delivery room,

your hospital room or even at home. Don't be afraid the bond will be weaker if you cannot "meet in the delivery room."

The hour following birth is a prime bonding time for mom, dad and baby. Mother and infant are programmed to connect at this time. Both need each other. The mother needs to see, touch, smell and hold this person she has carried for 9 months. The baby needs the comfort of her mother's touch after going through the stressful birth process.

FAST FACTS

There may be a physical aspect to bonding. Some researchers believe bonding stimulates production of the hormones prolactin and oxytocin in you, which cause you to feel more motherly toward your baby.

Bonding often begins in the delivery room. Ask if procedures normally done can safely be postponed for a little while so you can share this time together. If you can't hold your baby, ask your partner or a nurse to hold the baby up to your face, where you can nuzzle her with your cheek. Bonding can continue in your hospital room, if you have baby in your room. You can respond to your baby as soon as she begins to cry or to make noises.

Breastfeeding is one of the best ways to bond with your baby, especially if you feed her on demand. You can respond to your baby whenever she needs you. If you do not breastfeed, you can bond when you bottlefeed. Respond to your baby when she cries. Look at her, talk to her and hold her close. Create as much skin-to-skin contact as possible. As your infant begins to mature, this bonding process will be strengthened. Relax and let it happen.

Dads can bond with baby, too. Encourage dad to hold the baby close, like you do, and to make eye contact and skin contact. He can respond just as you do to the baby's cries. Let him feed baby when you begin expressing your breast milk.

The key to bonding is to focus on the baby and the experiences you share. Include baby in your daily activities. For example, if

you're ironing or doing the dishes, put her in her infant carrier and keep her close to you. Talk to her, or sing silly songs. Holding, cuddling and cooing are great ways to bond. Your baby will connect with you because she feels the love and security you offer.

S O S

Make your appointment for your 6-week postpartum checkup as soon as you get home from the hospital. Keep the appointment! It's a very important visit with your doctor so you can discuss resuming activities, birth control and future pregnancies.

VISITS TO THE DOCTOR

Most doctors want you to come in for an exam following a C-section or a postpartum tubal ligation 10 to 14 days after you leave the hospital. The doctor will examine the incision to see if it is healing properly and to look for signs of infection. A pelvic exam is usually *not* done at this visit.

The doctor will ask if you are having any problems, such as bleeding, pain, problems with breastfeeding, difficult bowel movements or problems with your bladder function. If you were anemic after delivery, you may need a blood test.

Your body changes a lot during the next 4 to 6 weeks. By the time you visit your doctor for your 6-week postpartum checkup, your uterus will be about the size of a grapefruit. That's incredible, considering it was the size of a small watermelon only a few short weeks before!

Your doctor will check your weight and blood pressure. A pelvic exam will be done to check your vagina, uterus and cervix to see how healing has progressed. Your breasts may also be checked.

If you had a vaginal birth, your doctor will examine any tears or incisions you had. If you had a C-section, your incision will be examined. If you developed hemorrhoids or varicose veins during pregnancy, your doctor will check those, too.

If you have any questions about your recovery, be sure to address them at this time with your physician. It's a good time to discuss birth-control options if you do not want to become pregnant again immediately.

2

After Your Baby's Birth

Your hospital stay allows you to relax and to regroup before you go home with your baby. Take advantage of the resources available to you there. Learn as much as you can about what to expect after delivery. Listen to and follow the advice of your doctor and the nurses at the hospital. Take good care of yourself so that you heal quickly.

Whether you had a vaginal or Cesarean delivery, you are checked closely for the first few hours following the birth and are offered medication to relieve pain. As you recover in your room, your urine output may be checked to ensure your kidneys and bladder are working. Nurses check your incision, if you had an episiotomy or a Cesarean, to make sure it heals properly. Your blood pressure, the amount of bleeding and other things will be monitored as you recover.

The nursing staff is available to help you if you have questions about your care or the care of your baby. Nurses are often very knowledgeable about breastfeeding and are happy to help you begin.

They can also show you how to care for your baby, such as bathing or diapering him. They will advise you how to deal with your episiotomy and care for your breasts. They also allow you to rest—something you probably need very much!

Eat a good meal, if you're hungry. Your body needs a well-balanced, nutritious diet for you to stay healthy and to keep your energy level up. Drink lots of fluids.

You will probably experience two main areas of pain—your abdomen and your episiotomy (if you had one). Pain medication will help with both; if your doctor does not offer it to you, ask about it, even if you are nursing.

Most women are discharged within a day or two after their baby's birth, if labor and delivery were normal and the baby is doing well.

....

FAST FACTS

Some researchers believe that emotional tears play a part in helping the body deal with stress. If you feel like a good cry, do it!

....

AFTER-PREGNANCY CHANGES

Your skin may have gone through various changes during pregnancy. You may have developed acne, even if you never had it before. It's a way the body reacts to fluctuating hormones; your skin should begin to clear up now. Or you may develop acne after your baby is born. If this occurs, over-the-counter topical medication can help. If you don't breastfeed, your doctor may prescribe acne medication for you.

Freckles and moles sometimes darken and enlarge during pregnancy. You may have noticed darkened pigment, called *chloasma* or the *mask of pregnancy,* around your nose, cheek-bones, forehead, upper lip and eyes. It usually fades within 6 months after delivery. Skin tags may have appeared during pregnancy, or they may appear after birth. These small growths of skin are easily removed by a physician.

Stretch marks are scars left where the skin stretched during pregnancy. Some women have few stretch marks caused by pregnancy. Others have severe stretch marks caused by weight gain and hormones that allow the skin's elastic fibers to relax and stretch. They are probably purple red at this time, but they will gradually fade to silver white lines in a year or so.

....

FAST FACTS

You may be disappointed if you're expecting to lose 30 or 40 pounds immediately after baby's birth. It takes awhile for things to get back to normal, so be patient.

....

The areola, the area around the nipple, may darken and enlarge slightly. This may occur as a signal to the breastfeeding infant. Discoloration usually lightens a few months after the birth, although the areolas may be darker than before pregnancy.

If the *linea nigra*—the dark line of pigmentation that runs from your belly button down to the pubis symphysis—darkened, it will fade after a few months. But it may never disappear completely.

Your sense of smell may have been more acute during pregnancy. This heightened sensitivity usually begins to fade 6 or 8 weeks after the birth.

If your gums bled more easily during pregnancy, they should get better now. Keep flossing and brushing your teeth regularly. You might want to schedule a dental cleaning and an exam.

Swelling in your legs, hands or feet lessens or disappears within a couple of weeks. Varicose veins may disappear, but spider veins may be permanent.

If your fingernails and toenails grew rapidly during pregnancy, growth will probably return to normal within a couple of weeks. Nails may even become brittle after your baby's birth.

....

FAST FACTS

After delivery, following a normal pregnancy, your body retains about 3 quarts (3 liters) of water. It can take several weeks to get rid of this extra fluid.

....

TUBAL LIGATION

Some women choose to have a form of surgical sterilization performed, called *tubal ligation* or *getting your tubes tied*, while they are in the hospital after their baby's birth. The surgery prevents further pregnancies by making it impossible for a sperm and egg to unite. If you haven't thought seriously about it before, this is *not* the time to make a decision about a tubal ligation.

SOS

 If you're considering tubal ligation after your baby's birth, talk to your doctor about it before pregnancy or early in your pregnancy. Consider the procedure irreversible.

If you have already decided before baby's birth to have a tubal ligation, doing it after delivery, while you're still in the hospital, can make sense. If you received an epidural for your labor and delivery, you are already anesthetized for a tubal ligation. If you didn't have an epidural, in most cases the procedure requires general anesthesia.

There are disadvantages to having a tubal ligation immediately after your baby's birth. You must consider the surgery permanent and irreversible. If you have your tubes tied within a few hours or a day after having your baby, then change your mind, you may regret it.

FAST FACTS

The failure rate for tubal ligation is 1 to 2 in 1,000 procedures. Failure rates are a little higher for tubal ligations performed immediately after delivery than when performed at other times.

RECOVERY FROM A VAGINAL BIRTH

Frequently a doctor hears new parents remark in relief, "It's over!" following delivery of their baby. It's true the long months of pregnancy and the labor and delivery are over, but another very exciting and perhaps more challenging part of life has just begun!

In the Hospital

One of the first things you may notice after delivery is how tired you are. Some women have compared their feeling of exhaustion to how a person feels after running a marathon.

After the excitement of the birth passes, it isn't unusual to be worn out. Rest and recover while you're in the hospital. Take advantage of the "built-in" room service and babysitting provided in the hospital. You probably won't have this luxury when you go home, especially if you have young children.

For the first hour after delivery, the nurses will check you frequently for bleeding, pain, fever, blood-pressure problems and other warning signs while you and your partner bond with your new baby. The baby is also being evaluated.

During this time you will probably only be allowed ice chips and sips of water, even though you may be anxious to eat some food and to drink some fluids. Restriction of food and drink is for your safety; if there are problems, such as heavy bleeding (postpartum hemorrhage), it is sometimes necessary to perform minor surgery, such as a D&C. It is safer for you to have your stomach empty if this procedure is necessary.

Dealing with Contractions, Pain and Bleeding

You may have thought that once you delivered, contractions would disappear. Your uterus actually continues to contract. These contractions are important because they cause your uterus to shrink to its normal size and help prevent excessive bleeding. Nursing your baby makes contractions stronger and helps control bleeding.

Another source of discomfort after you deliver will be in the vagina and between the opening of the vagina and the rectum. This is the area where an episiotomy was done or where tearing may have occurred with the delivery of the baby's head or shoulders. You will be offered medicine and ice packs to help with pain and swelling. Your nurse will show you how to take care of this area while you are in the hospital and when you go home.

Medication is available to help with contractions and pain. It is not given routinely; it is ordered for you and all you have to do is ask for it. Initially pain medicine may be in the form of an injection until you are allowed to drink and to eat. After that, you will usually be offered pain pills, such as ibuprofen or acetaminophen, as well as stronger pain medications, such as Tylenol #3.

It's normal to bleed for several days up to a couple of weeks after delivery. Your nurses and doctor will check your bleeding to make sure it is not excessive. After delivery, bleeding should gradually slow down, but you will still be bleeding when you go home from the hospital. Most often, medication is given to you at the time of delivery of the baby, by I.V. or injection, to help your uterus contract to prevent excessive bleeding.

If there is concern about infection, you may be given antibiotics. If bleeding is excessive, you may be given vitamins and iron. If you are Rh-negative, you may be given RhoGAM®.

Laxatives and stool softeners may be prescribed to help avoid constipation. An enema at the beginning of labor may also help lessen the problem of a painful bowel movement after delivery.

Passing urine may be uncomfortable, or it may hurt. This discomfort usually doesn't last very long and doesn't necessarily mean you have a bladder or urinary-tract infection (UTI). Just take it easy, and take your time when you have to go to the bathroom.

Meeting Visitors

Friends and family will probably want to visit you in the hospital. This time can be enjoyable for everyone and can be very valuable for you and for them. But don't be afraid to limit the time spent with visitors—either in person or on the telephone. Put a hold on your phone calls or hang a "Do not disturb" sign on your door when you want to rest. Ask visitors to check with the nurses before coming into your room. Most people are very understanding about this, particularly if they have also had a baby.

Going Home

Before you leave the hospital, your doctor and pediatrician will talk to you about making appointments for checkups for you and your baby. These appointments are very important, so be sure to keep them.

When you leave the hospital, you will still be bleeding, but the amount of bloody discharge should be decreasing. Sometimes when you go home and are more active, bleeding may be a little heavier at first, but this shouldn't last more than a few hours before it slows down again.

It is normal to have cramps or pain in the area of the episiotomy. Discomfort should lessen every day. Usually you will be given a prescription for mild pain medications. It's OK to take these medicines, but usually they are not needed as often once you are home.

You may want to continue to take prenatal vitamins or iron. Many doctors will encourage you to take stool softeners or laxatives, as already discussed.

Resuming Activities

If you had an epidural, it takes a few hours for it to wear off before you are able to get out of bed. Within a few hours, you'll be able to get out of bed and walk around or go to the bathroom. Don't try to do too much. Most doctors don't want you just to sit in bed (we often describe this as "sitting in bed watching TV, eating bon-bons and taking pain pills"). Get out of bed and go for a walk, but don't push it at this time.

When you go home, gradually increase your activities. You can walk around, eat more normally and become more active each day. You may also feel like you need to rest frequently—that's normal. Pay attention to your body. Most doctors recommend you wait until your 6-week postpartum checkup before you begin any strenuous activity or exercise or become sexually active again.

Many women ask about driving and going up and down stairs. If you're still taking pain medicines or are having problems, such as dizziness, don't drive. It's OK to use stairs, but plan ahead so you're not running up and down the stairs all day. Park yourself where you are comfortable, are close to the baby and have food and beverages near at hand.

Taking Precautions

The nurses and your doctor will go over any precautions before you go home. This includes instructions about normal bleeding and what to do about pain. If you have any problems, it's helpful when you call your doctor to give information about bleeding, such as how many pads you are using, if there are there clots and what you have done or what you have taken to help deal with the problem. See the list on page 30.

Getting Back on Your Feet

Full recovery is different for every woman, but there are some basic guidelines. If you had complications or problems, it may be different for you. From 2 to 6 weeks, you should be feeling a little better every day. You probably won't be taking pain medicine any longer, and bleeding will be decreasing or will have stopped. You have a full-time job taking care of your newborn, but you should be able to find some time for yourself and for your partner.

Following a normal pregnancy and delivery, the 6-week postpartum checkup is usually a turning point. Talk to your doctor about contraception. You'll probably get an OK to resume routine activities, such as exercise, sexual intercourse or returning to work.

If you are returning to work, make plans *weeks* before you start working again for childcare, nursing and your own recovery. You need to decide whether you are going to work full time or part time. See Chapter 9 for a discussion on returning to the workplace.

· ·

FAST FACTS

If you can't rest during the day when your baby sleeps, go to bed earlier at night to get some rest.

· ·

Taking Care of Baby

In the first 24 hours after delivery, you and your baby will probably still be in the hospital. Your baby's pediatrician will come to the hospital to do a physical on the baby, then see you to discuss making an office appointment. If you have a boy, the pediatrician will talk to you about circumcision. Your signature is required before this procedure can be done. In some hospitals, your obstetrician will do this, while in other areas, it is done by the pediatrician or family practitioner.

While you are in the hospital, much of your time is spent getting to know your baby. You thought it was difficult to sleep at night during the pregnancy because you were uncomfortable. At least then you didn't have to feed someone or change any diapers!

At home, during the first week after birth, you will probably try to establish some kind of schedule for you and your baby. Don't be surprised if the baby isn't a willing participant; this can take weeks or months. During this time, try to nap or rest whenever you can. When your baby sleeps, take a rest. Try to avoid the temptation to catch up on your housework or other tasks.

The first 6 months after delivery may seem like hard work. It is a challenging time but also very enjoyable and rewarding. As your baby grows and starts to react to you and to your partner, it is a wonderful time of your life. Enjoy it. It is also a time of many changes. If you work outside of the home, you will be going back to work. If you exercise, each week you should see results.

During the first year, you spend a lot of time with your baby and a lot of energy caring for the baby, but you should be able to find time for yourself. This may take some effort; you may want to trade babysitting with another new mom on a regular basis so that you can exercise or participate in other activities you like.

By the end of the first year after delivery, you will have this "baby thing" down. A sure sign of this achievement is that you may even be talking about another pregnancy.

FAST FACTS

About 80% of all women have baby blues after giving birth; the feelings usually appear sometime in the first 4 to 6 weeks after the baby is born.

RECOVERY FROM A CESAREAN DELIVERY

There are many similarities in recovering from a vaginal delivery and a Cesarean delivery. However, there are some distinct differences you should be aware of if you had a C-section.

In the Hospital

Immediately after your C-section, you are taken to a recovery room or recovery area for about an hour. Here you will be watched for any signs of problems, such as bleeding or pain. Your blood pressure and other vital signs, such as pulse and temperature, are checked frequently. At this same time, your baby may go to the nursery to be weighed and evaluated, but he is often returned to you while you are still in the recovery room. This is a good time to begin nursing your baby. When you leave recovery, you will go to a room where you will spend the remainder of your time in the hospital.

How long a woman stays in the hospital after a Cesarean delivery varies quite a bit. Most women stay for 2 to 4 days after delivery. Your insurance company or HMO has the greatest say about this, not you or your doctor. An average stay is 3 days after a C-section.

S O S

 If the incision from your C-section gets red, oozes pus or yellow fluid, bleeds or becomes painful, call your doctor.

Dealing with Contractions, Pain and Bleeding

Cramping and contraction of your uterus are normal and desirable after a C-section. Contractions of the uterus help control and decrease bleeding after your delivery. With a C-section, there is pain from the surgery itself, but at least you won't have episiotomy pain.

Pain control after a Cesarean is accomplished in different ways. If you had an epidural or spinal anesthetic for the surgery, you may be able to have pain medicine injected through the epidural or spinal catheter; this is called *Duramorph* or *epidural morphine*. Medication usually offers pain relief for the first 24 hours and helps you avoid painful injections or pain pills for the first day after surgery.

Other choices for pain relief are those traditionally used following surgery, such as injections of pain medications (Demerol or morphine) through an I.V. or into a muscle during the first 24 hours after delivery until you are able to eat. Once you're able to eat, you may be offered oral pain medications, such as mild narcotics (Tylenol #3 or Lortab) or anti-inflammatory pain medications, such as ibuprofen.

It is normal to bleed vaginally after a Cesarean; this continues for several days up to a few weeks. It should decrease each day. The nurses will check to see it is not excessive and instruct you what to look for after you go home.

If you were in labor for a long time before delivery, you may be exhausted. Get some rest so you're ready for the challenges awaiting you at home. Don't be afraid to accept help or suggestions from the nurses or others at the hospital. There are specific areas the nurses can help you with and teach you about, such as nursing, caring for your baby and warning signs of problems when you go home.

Meeting Visitors

Greeting visitors who come to see you in the hospital (actually they really come to see the baby!) can be most enjoyable. Set aside some quiet time for you and the baby, though; use the time to recover somewhat before you go home.

Dealing with Inconveniences

In most cases with a C-section, a catheter is placed in your bladder through the urethra (the small tube from the bladder to the outside) to keep the bladder empty and out of the way during surgery. The catheter is usually left in place for 12 to 24 hours after the surgery. This is something to talk to your doctor about if you are planning a C-section or after the surgery, if it is unplanned. Different doctors handle it in different ways.

Problems with gas or bowel movements are more common following a C-section than with a vaginal delivery, but there are things you can do to minimize them. Get up and walk around as soon as possible. You may need help with this at first. Drink plenty of liquids; this is more important than trying to eat solid foods in the first few days after delivery. Sitting in bed and taking pain medications, vitamins or iron can all cause changes or problems with your bowels.

The sooner you get moving, stop taking pain medications and start eating a more normal diet, the sooner your bowels will return to normal. Laxatives or stool softeners are available, if necessary. Although it may seem unpleasant, passing gas is a good sign that your bowels are working.

The doctor and nurses will check your C-section incision daily for infection or bleeding while you are in the hospital. If staples were used on the incision, they are usually removed before you leave the hospital on the second or third postoperative day. This may seem a little soon, but don't worry; the layers of tissue that really hold you together are deeper. Deeper sutures will dissolve on their own, but that takes weeks or even months. If sutures were used to close the skin over your abdomen, they may have to be removed or they may dissolve on their own. Most doctors place Steri-strips (like small pieces of tape) on the incision that stay on for 3 or 4 days. Before you leave the hospital, the nurses will show you how to take care of the incision and advise you of warning signs to watch for when you go home.

Going Home

When you go home from the hospital, you will be eating, drinking and walking. Your incision is likely to be sore, and you will still be bleeding vaginally. Most women need mild pain medication after they go home; you will be offered prescriptions before you leave the hospital. Sometimes pain or bleeding increases when you increase your activities. However, you should see an overall decrease in pain and bleeding every day.

Your doctor will recommend that you not drive if you are taking pain medicine or have other problems, such as anemia. You may not want to drive for a few weeks, if you are uncomfortable or have trouble getting in or out of your car.

Resuming Activities

It's OK to increase your activity gradually, but try not to be in too big a hurry. Usually friends or family are more than happy to help out. Let them! Save your energy to take care of yourself and your baby. This includes stairs—plan ahead! If you're running up and down the stairs all day, chances are you will have more pain and tire more easily.

Certain activities may not be a good idea because of increased pain, or they may cause complications and slow down your recovery. During the first few weeks, don't lift anything heavier than your baby. Vacuuming probably isn't going to be harmful, but it may cause you discomfort because of the stretching or pulling.

Don't start exercising or resume sexual relations. Most doctors will want to see you in the office 10 to 14 days after your C-section to check your incision and see how you're doing. This visit is a good time to ask how soon you can safely resume activities and what level of exercise is appropriate for you.

From week 2 to week 6, you will notice gradual improvements in your energy every day. By 6 weeks, you can usually do anything you want. In the months to come you may not see big changes, but you will experience subtle improvements.

Taking Precautions

Most doctors suggest that you don't have sexual relations until after your 6-week postpartum visit. In most cases, you won't be ready for relations before this time because you're still bleeding, in pain or tired. Resuming relations too soon can be harmful because of possible infection or increased bleeding. This kind of activity may delay your recovery.

Wait to start exercising until *after* your doctor gives you the go-ahead. You can gradually increase your activity, but don't try anything strenuous or uncomfortable until your doctor approves of your exercise plans at the 6-week postpartum visit.

Your doctor will explain what warning signs to be alert for, such as pain, bleeding, fever or signs of infection. If you feel that something is not right, call your doctor's office—he or she expects this and has specific people to help you with problems. Good sources of information include the nurses in the birthing center or hospital where you delivered or the emergency room. Many areas have nurses available 24 hours a day who you can call for advice.

Getting Back on Your Feet

The rate of recovery from a Cesarean delivery is different for every woman. Usually you can return to your normal activities after your 6-week checkup, if you're not having problems. Be prepared to go slowly. A C-section is surgery that requires an abdominal incision. Besides the normal recovery from surgery, you have a full-time job (night and day) caring for your baby!

When you go home from the hospital, you'll be able to get in and out of bed on your own and you will be walking. Certain activities, such as bending or lifting, may be uncomfortable; take things slowly. Your recovery will be smoother if you take care of yourself, rest when necessary and increase activities gradually.

Taking Care of Baby

Most new parents feel overwhelmed and inadequate with their new responsibility. Be assured—you'll do great and learn as you go! There are many ways to get help—friends, family, your pediatrician's office and even people you meet in the hospital. Care of your baby after a C-section should be the same as the care required following a vaginal delivery. As the weeks pass, you will settle into a routine at home for feeding, sleeping and caring for your baby.

3

Now What Happens?

You've just had your baby, and everything is great . . . isn't it? You can probably answer "yes" to that question, but you may have other questions about the postpartum recovery period. These concerns are normal—nearly every woman wonders about some of them. Your "problems" are normal, too, whether they are physical or emotional.

You may want to read all the topics in this chapter, or you may want to read only about those you are interested in. We have tried to give you information to reassure you that what you experience is not unusual. If you have questions about any of this information or if you are concerned about your particular situation, call your doctor. He or she is there to answer your questions and to reassure you.

SOME WARNING SIGNS

Things should go well for you after your baby's birth—you shouldn't feel ill. However, you might occasionally experience a problem. Below is a list of symptoms and warning signs to be alert for. If you experience any of these symptoms, call your doctor. It's important information to share with him or her. Your doctor may want to see you and a course of treatment may be prescribed for you. Be alert for:

- temperature of 101F (38.3C) or more, except in the first 24 hours after birth

- painful or red breasts

- chills

- loss of appetite for an extended period

- pain in the lower abdomen or in the back

- pain, tenderness, redness and/or swelling in your legs

- painful urination or feeling an intense need to urinate

- failure to pass gas or severe constipation (no bowel movements for a few days)

- severe pain in the vagina or perineum area

- unusually heavy bleeding or a sudden increase in bleeding (more than your normal menstrual flow or soaking more than two sanitary pads in 30 minutes)

- vaginal discharge with strong, unpleasant odor

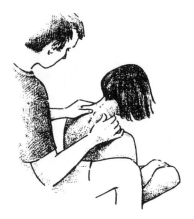

TREAT YOURSELVES WELL

Getting back into the swing of things as a couple after pregnancy and delivery can take some planning on your part. You need to be creative to handle the demands on your time and energies, and to reward yourselves occasionally. Think about ways you can pamper yourself and your partner. The following suggestions may help you make your lives together, and as a family, more enjoyable.

Take care of yourself at home. Find some quiet time for yourself. When your partner can tend the baby, treat yourself to a long soak in the tub or spend some time alone reading or doing crafts. You may want to get out of the house to do a bit of shopping or to meet a friend for lunch. Allow your partner some time to himself, too. He may want to work on a project, do some research on the computer or play a game of golf. When each of you is allowed time alone, you renew your inner strength and your commitment to your life as a couple.

Pamper yourselves as a couple. Do something special for yourselves when you can. Order a great dinner from a good restaurant (we're not talking fast food here). Set the table with your good dishes, add flowers and candles, and maybe a glass of wine. Dress nicely. Plan to sit down and eat after you put baby down. Take your time, and make your dinner as romantic as you can. It's your special time together. Another suggestion is to hire a sitter or ask friends or family members to take care of baby while you go to a movie, a play or a concert. A couple of hours away from the house and baby allows you to renew your relationship.

Massage is good for your soul. Each of you can learn some massage techniques to help the other relax. There are some excellent books and videos available to check out at the library or to rent or buy at a video store that provide instructions on "couple massage." We're not talking about anything sexual; the techniques we recommend are for relaxation and stress reduction.

Ask for, and accept, help from friends and family. When someone wants to help you, let them! If they ask how they can help, there are many things you can ask them to do. Ready-made meals to put in the refrigerator or freezer to eat later are always welcome. Cleaning services and laundry help are great gifts. You may be grateful if someone can watch the baby while you rest or take care of other tasks. Tending your baby is especially helpful if you have other children and want to spend some time with them.

Be creative. If you have personal needs, ask someone to help you meet them. If you don't have family near and your friends are unable to help you during the day, consider hiring someone to do various chores for you.

SOS

 If you took any medication before or during pregnancy, ask your doctor about continuing it or resuming it after delivery.

SOME HEALTH PRECAUTIONS

If you have a chronic illness, such as diabetes or asthma, it may affect your recovery. You may need to watch for specific problems or to make particular adjustments. You may need to take medications or to adjust your activities; check with your doctor about your particular situation.

For example, if you had gestational diabetes during pregnancy, your blood-sugar level may need to be tested after delivery. Discuss results with your doctor. If your blood-sugar level is normal, you're OK. If it isn't, you may be referred to a doctor who specializes in treating diabetes. He or she can help you plan a program to deal with your problem. Most of the time delivery cures gestational diabetes, and you are fine until you are pregnant again, when it may recur. Gestational diabetes may also indicate a tendency in a woman for diabetes to occur later in life, so you may wish to ask your doctor about warning signs to watch for.

....

FAST FACTS

After delivery, the uterus shrinks from the size of a watermelon to the size of an orange in 6 weeks!

....

CHANGES IN THE UTERUS

After baby's birth, your uterus slowly returns to its original shape. Just before birth, the uterus was large enough to accommodate the baby, placenta and amniotic fluid. Immediately after delivery, you should feel your uterus around your navel; it should be very hard. You are checked frequently to make sure it remains hard after delivery. If it feels soft, you or a nurse can massage it so it becomes firm.

The uterus shrinks about a finger's width every day; this is called *involution*. You will be checked daily while you're in the hospital to ensure that your uterus is shrinking normally. This exam can be a little uncomfortable, but it is necessary for normal control of bleeding.

AFTERPAINS

Afterpains are just what they sound like—pains you experience after the birth of your baby. They are normal; expect to feel them for several days after birth as your uterus contracts. Contractions occur to prevent heavy bleeding and to enable the uterus to return to its normal size. Cramps can be eased by lying on your stomach and by taking mild pain relievers, such as acetaminophen or ibuprofen.

If you breastfeed, your afterpains may intensify when you nurse. The baby's sucking stimulates the pituitary gland to release oxytocin, which makes the uterus contract. These extra contractions are good for you because they help control bleeding, but they can be uncomfortable. Mild pain medication can offer relief.

PERINEUM PAIN

Stretching, cutting or tearing in the area between the vagina and anus during labor and delivery can cause pain in the perineum. An episiotomy can add to this discomfort. Pain doesn't last too long; soreness should diminish daily and disappear in about 3 weeks or by the time you see your doctor for your 6-week checkup.

If you experience severe discomfort, use ice packs, which may offer some relief in the first 24 hours after delivery. Ice numbs the area and helps reduce swelling. After 24 hours, a warm bath or soaking in a sitz tub several times a day can help.

Other remedies for pain include numbing sprays, witch-hazel compresses, walking to stimulate circulation and practicing your Kegel exercises. Pads soaked in hemorrhoid medication (sold over the counter) can be kept in the freezer, then placed on the sore area—they provide excellent relief.

Urinating may be painful because urine can sting the cut area. This burning is not an indication of a UTI or bladder infection. It is caused by the chemicals in the urine that cause stinging along the cut. You may find it less painful to urinate standing or in the shower with running water washing over the area.

FAST FACTS

It may seem like you're bleeding a lot during and after delivery, but remember, your blood volume increased 50% during pregnancy, so you have extra blood in your body.

BLEEDING AFTER DELIVERY

It's common to lose some blood during labor and delivery. However, heavy bleeding after the baby is born can be a concern. A loss of more than 17 ounces (500ml) in the first 24 hours after your baby's birth is called *postpartum hemorrhage*.

The most common causes of heavy bleeding include the following:

- when your uterus doesn't contract
- a large or bleeding episiotomy
- clotting or coagulation problems
- failure of blood vessels inside the uterus to compress
- retained placental tissue or retained blood clots in the uterus
- rips or tears in the vagina or cervix from the birth
- a tear, rupture or hole in the uterus (rare)

Bleeding is controlled by massaging the uterus (called *Credé*) and use of certain medications, such as Pitocin or methergine. The normal bleeding after delivery, lochia, gradually decreases each day until it stops. It may become a little heavier when you increase your activities.

If bleeding suddenly becomes heavy after a few days or weeks, contact your doctor. He or she may want to see you to prescribe medication.

YOUR CHANGING BOWEL HABITS

Your bowel habits will probably change for a few days after your baby's birth. Your digestive system slows down during labor and after delivery because of medications, such as pain pills, because of changes in your activity level or because you sit or lie in bed. You may have had an enema, or the lower part of your bowel (the rectum) may have emptied while you pushed during labor and delivery. These factors can all contribute to bowel-habit changes.

Many women don't want to have to deal with having a bowel movement for the first 4 or 5 days after delivery because it hurts. Some new mothers have said that their first bowel movement after delivery felt like they were delivering another baby.

If you had an episiotomy or if you have hemorrhoids, your bowel movements may be more difficult or more painful. You may be apprehensive about having one. Now is not the time to be constipated. To avoid constipation, eat a high-fiber diet and drink lots of fluids to keep your system working efficiently.

Prune juice and bran are natural laxatives; include them in your diet. Over-the-counter stool softeners may also be beneficial. Many stool softeners and laxatives are safe to use if you breastfeed. If you don't have a bowel movement within a week or if you become uncomfortable, contact your doctor.

When you do have a bowel movement, try not to strain. This can aggravate hemorrhoids or make an episiotomy incision or the area of a laceration hurt or bleed. Hemorrhoids eventually shrink on their own, although they may not go away completely. A witch-hazel compress or a commercial compress can offer relief. Over-the-counter creams and ointments and mild pain medication and anti-inflammatories, such as ibuprofen, can also offer some relief. Ice packs may help. More serious measures are usually unnecessary.

CHANGES IN YOUR BREASTS

Whether you breastfeed or bottlefeed, sore breasts are fairly common after delivery. In the natural course of pregnancy and delivery, your body has prepared you to breastfeed, so your breasts will fill with milk.

The fullness of milk in your breasts, called *engorgement*, usually lasts a few days and may be uncomfortable. If you breastfeed, you can empty your breasts when the baby nurses, and the situation resolves itself in a few days. It's a little more difficult for a woman who chooses not to breastfeed because breast milk still comes in. Medication is no longer given to stop the production of breast milk. You can ease discomfort by wearing a support bra or binding your breasts with an Ace® bandage or a towel. Ice packs also help milk dry up.

If you find your breasts are engorged, and you are not breast-feeding, try *not* to empty your breasts. This may be difficult; emptying your breasts may be the only way to get relief. However, when you empty your breasts, your body replaces the expressed breast milk with more milk! Avoid nipple stimulation and warm water on the breasts because these practices also stimulate milk production. Hearing a baby cry—yours or some-one else's—may also make you lose milk.

A mild fever with engorgement is not uncommon. Acetaminophen can help with both the fever and the discom-fort from engorgement. For information on problems associated with breastfeeding, such as plugged milk ducts and breast infec-tions, see Chapter 4.

URINARY INCONTINENCE

Bladder function or voiding urine may be different after delivery for many reasons. During labor and afterward, fluids are often given by I.V. for various reasons. Oxytocin (Pitocin), given dur-ing or after labor, has an "antidiuretic" effect; it causes a de-crease in urine production. Once this effect has passed, you have a lot of fluid to get rid of—you'll need to urinate a lot! Bladder sensation can also be affected by pain from delivery, a tear in the birth canal or anesthesia, such as an epidural.

Some women have trouble controlling their urine after birth; this condition is called *urinary incontinence*. This may last briefly, or it can last a few weeks or longer. Most women report that the more pregnancies and deliveries they have, the greater their problem with incontinence. There are several factors that contribute to this, including the size of the baby, the number of deliveries, the size of the uterus, your age and whether you had a vaginal delivery or a C-section.

For a baby's head and shoulders to fit through the birth canal, your muscles and connective tissues stretch a great deal. Your bladder lies in front of the uterus, and the lower part of the bladder wall is stretched during birth. After delivery, this area is weaker than before pregnancy, which can contribute to incontinence. Each delivery stretches the birth canal. Tissues that support the bladder are also stretched with each delivery, causing some incontinence.

It takes a few weeks or more for your uterus to return to normal size. In the weeks immediately after delivery, the uterus gradually contracts and grows smaller, and it lies directly on the bladder. This compresses your bladder so it won't hold as much urine. It might be harder for you to control urine loss.

You can help yourself regain bladder and urine control by practicing Kegel exercises. Do not hold your urine; empty your bladder fairly often. It takes time for things to get better. Chances are that your bladder control may not be the same as before you became pregnant.

Let your doctor know if a urinary incontinence problem continues or worsens. Improvement may not come for weeks after delivery, until you begin to get back in shape. Surgery may help, but most doctors prefer to perform this kind of surgery only when you are finished having children. Any further pregnancies may undo the benefits of the surgery.

VARICOSE VEINS

Varicose veins, blood vessels that are dilated or enlarged, are a fairly common result of pregnancy. They are also called *varicosities*. You may have an inherited predisposition to varicose veins—if your mother had them, you have a greater chance of having them, too.

Varicose veins occur most often in the legs, but they may also occur in the vulva and vagina. Varicosities will not disappear immediately after delivery. Follow the tips you were given during pregnancy to help deal with varicose veins after your baby is born. Some of these tips include the following:

- Lie on your side (left is best) as much as possible.
- Elevate your legs above the level of your heart when you can.
- Don't wear restrictive clothing.
- Get up and walk throughout the day.
- Don't cross your legs.
- Get regular exercise.
- Don't stand for long periods.

Symptoms can range from cosmetic blemishes to mild to moderate pain. Discomfort is usually more pronounced at the end of the day or after a day spent standing or walking a lot. Occasionally *superficial thrombophlebitis* (blood clots) in these veins can be a problem during or after pregnancy. Clots can be painful but are not dangerous; they don't travel to other parts of the body.

In severe cases, varicose veins may require treatment, including injection, ligation, stripping and laser treatment. It is rare to perform any of these procedures until you are finished childbearing.

SWELLING AND WATER RETENTION

Swelling and water retention are a normal part of pregnancy. Water retention occurs because of hormonal changes and the blockage of blood flow by the enlarging uterus. Because it takes weeks for your uterus to return to its prepregnancy size, it takes some time to get rid of this extra water.

To help lessen swelling, do the same things you were advised to do during pregnancy. Lie on your side several times during the day and at night when you sleep. Get up and get moving; if you just sit in bed, it'll take longer to get rid of extra fluid. Elevating your legs above the level of your heart can help, but lying on your side is better. Exercise regularly.

HEADACHES

Headaches can be a problem for some women after delivery. They don't usually indicate a problem, but they can make you miserable. Headaches can be caused or influenced by many factors—for example, a long labor, having to push for a while or if you have not slept in 24 to 36 hours. If you had pre-eclampsia or pregnancy-induced hypertension, either could cause a headache.

Epidural anesthesia or a spinal anesthetic for labor or a C-section can result in a headache called a *spinal headache*. It doesn't happen often—once in every 100 deliveries—and is treated with bed rest and fluids. Sometimes an epidural blood patch is used to seal the area of leakage from the spinal canal. With this procedure, blood is withdrawn from your arm and introduced into the spinal canal. You are advised to lie flat on your back for 2 to 3 hours, so the blood placed in the spinal area can clot and seal off any opening that may be causing the leakage. This procedure often helps stop the headache.

Occasionally, dealing with visitors and your new baby may contribute to a headache. If you have headaches, discuss the situation with your doctor. He or she can recommend a course of treatment for you. Usually rest, fluids and mild pain medicine offer relief. It's important to tell your doctor if you have a headache that doesn't go away or doesn't get better, especially if a headache is severe or is accompanied by blurred vision, headache or nausea.

EMOTIONS MAY CHANGE

You may experience many emotional changes after your baby is born. Mood swings, mild distress or bouts of crying are not uncommon. Changes in moods are often a result of hormonal changes you experience after birth, just as they were when you were pregnant. A lack of sleep may play a part in how you feel. Many women are surprised by how tired they are emotionally and physically in the first few months after their baby's birth. Make sure you take time for yourself. You'll have a period of adjustment.

Sleep and rest can help you deal with mood shifts, which seem to occur more often when a woman is exhausted. Taking care of yourself is very important. See the discussion below, and also see the discussion on postpartum distress syndrome, which begins on page 45.

GETTING ENOUGH SLEEP AND REST

Fatigue and exhaustion may become more of a problem after baby's birth. As many parents—both fathers and mothers—can tell you, it's no easy task to adjust to night after night of interrupted sleep. Now you have to do it all yourself—no nurses or hospital staff to help out! A baby usually wakes up every 2 to 4 hours to feed, which can be disruptive to her parents.

Don't be afraid to ask for help. Most people enjoy being called upon to help with a new baby. Your partner will want to help, but he may not know what to do. He may appreciate suggestions from you, such as getting up to feed the baby (this works best if you are not nursing) or bringing her to you for nursing in the middle of the night.

A cardinal rule with a newborn is "get sleep whenever and wherever you can." Until the baby is about 2 months old, you probably won't be able to put a long-term sleep plan into action. Some suggestions that might help include those below.

Involve Your Partner

Involve your partner in the decision about who's going to do what at night. If you're breastfeeding, your partner can change the baby's diaper then bring her to you. After your milk becomes established, he could feed the baby a bottle of expressed milk. If you are bottlefeeding, he can feed the baby on alternate nights.

Be Sure Baby Is Awake

Don't jump out of bed at your baby's first cry during the night. She may not really be awake or need tending. Give the baby a few minutes, and if she's still making noise, then go to her. You may be lucky and find she goes back to sleep without you having to get up.

Turn in Earlier

You might not be able to rest during the day when the baby sleeps, but going to bed earlier may be more easily accomplished. Don't stay up to watch the news or the late show. Go to bed around 8:30 or 9:00 pm, if possible. This may mean you have to let some things go, but that's OK if it allows you to get much-needed rest.

Get Daytime Help When Possible

The more support a couple has with daily tasks and chores, the easier it will be to deal with sleepless nights. Ask friends and family to help. They probably won't be offended and may be glad you asked them to pitch in.

Let things go when possible. The house doesn't have to be perfect, all the baby clothes and diapers don't have to be folded and put away, the kitchen doesn't always have to be spotless. Take it easy, and go easy on yourself.

Diaper Changes

Make it as simple as possible to take care of your baby during the middle of the night. Be sure baby's clothes are easy to work around. If a diaper isn't too wet, you may be able to let it go until the next feeding.

Exercise Every Day

Daily exercise can be helpful for you. Light exercise may help relieve some of the tension you feel and help you sleep. A stroll around the block can be very beneficial. When possible, take your partner and baby with you; make it a family affair.

IF YOU HAVE MORE THAN ONE BABY

Recovery after the birth of twins, triplets or more may be a little more difficult for several reasons. Your pregnancy may have been harder on your body than a singleton pregnancy. The risk of problems or complications is higher with a multiple pregnancy. You may have gained more weight or experienced more edema. You may have had a Cesarean delivery.

A multiple pregnancy usually delivers early, so you may not have had time to prepare to bring your babies home. Gestation for a singleton pregnancy is about 280 days. For twins, gestation is about 260 days, and for triplets, it is about 247 days.

Another problem with early delivery is prematurity of the babies. If your babies are premature and have to stay in the hospital, this can create emotional stress for you. An added stress is that you have two or more of everything—diapers to change, babies to feed, clothes to wash, little bodies to bathe.

It's important to ask for help from your partner, family and friends. Don't be shy about this. Many people are happy to help and are just waiting for you to ask. As you recover and the babies grow a little older and get on some kind of schedule, life will go more smoothly.

Be sure you get enough rest. Your body needs time to recover—probably even more time than if you only had one baby. Be kind to yourself. You'll be glad you did.

POSTPARTUM DISTRESS SYNDROME

After your baby is born, you may be surprised by some of the emotions you feel. You have waited so long for this wonderful new life and have anticipated feelings of great joy and happiness. You may be surprised if you find yourself feeling sad or unhappy. You have delivered your baby, and the anticipation and excitement are over. You may wonder if having a baby was a good idea. These feelings, called *postpartum distress*, are normal in up to 80% of all women after birth.

In the past, postpartum distress was called "postpartum depression," and the entire range of feelings a woman might experience was lumped together under that term. Today the general term is *postpartum distress syndrome*, and we distinguish between the intensity of the feelings.

Many women experience some degree of postpartum distress. Most of the time, feelings are mild; you may have heard them referred to as "baby blues." The situation is temporary and tends to leave as quickly as it comes. In unusual cases, it may last for several months and even more than a year.

Today, many experts consider some degree of postpartum distress normal. Some of the symptoms include:

- crying for no reason
- exhaustion
- irritability
- lack of confidence
- anxiety
- lack of feeling for the baby
- impatience
- low self-esteem
- oversensitivity
- restlessness

If you believe you are suffering from some of these symptoms, call your doctor. Almost all postpartum reactions are temporary and treatable.

S O S

If your baby blues don't get better in a few weeks, or if you feel extremely depressed, call your doctor. You may need medication to help deal with the problem.

Degrees of Postpartum Distress

The mildest form of postpartum distress is baby blues. This situation lasts only a couple of weeks, and symptoms do not worsen. (See the description above.) A more serious form of postpartum distress is called *postpartum depression* (PPD); it affects about 10% of all new mothers. The difference between baby blues and postpartum depression is in the frequency, intensity and duration of symptoms. Having problems sleeping is one way to distinguish between the two. If you can sleep while someone else tends the baby, it is probably baby blues. If you can't sleep because of anxiety, it may be PPD.

PPD can occur anytime from 2 weeks to 1 year after birth. A mother may have feelings of anger, confusion, panic and hopelessness. Her eating and sleeping patterns may change. She may be fearful she will hurt her baby or that she cannot take good care of the baby. She may think she is a bad mother or feel as if she is going crazy. Anxiety is a major symptom of PPD.

The most serious form of postpartum distress is called *postpartum psychosis*. In this situation, the woman may have hallucinations, think about suicide or try to harm the baby.

What Causes Postpartum Distress?

We don't know exactly what causes postpartum distress; not every woman experiences it. We believe hormonal changes are part of it. Many demands are placed on a new mother, which can cause distress. Other possible factors being considered include a family history of depression, little support after the birth, isolation and fatigue.

Ways to Deal with the Problem

You can help yourself in various ways. Begin before the baby's birth. Set up a support network; ask family members and friends to help. Have your mother or mother-in-law stay with you to help out for a while. Maybe your partner can take some leave from work. Consider hiring someone to come in to help each day. Realizing that many new moms experience these feelings is a step in the right direction.

There is no treatment for baby blues other than emotional support, but there are ways you can help ease symptoms. In addition to asking for help, rest when baby sleeps. Talk to your partner; it may be hard for him to support you if he doesn't know you're having a hard time. Find other mothers in the same situation; it helps to share your feelings and experiences. There may be some support groups in your area—ask your doctor for the names of groups. Keep the number of visitors to a small group. Entertaining guests can be exhausting and very stressful for you. Don't be too hard on yourself. Let some things slide. Take care of yourself. Exercise every day. Eat healthfully, drink plenty of fluids and avoid alcohol. Try to get out of the house every day.

With postpartum depression, the situation is a little more serious. Use the above suggestions. In addition, medication may be necessary to help relieve some symptoms. Research indicates about 85% of all women who suffer from postpartum depression require medication, including antidepressants, tranquilizers and hormones; often they are used together. No single treatment has been shown to be more effective than another.

If you breastfeed, medication selection may be more limited. Certain medications, such as Pamelor, Prozac and Norpramin, can be used by a woman while breastfeeding. The baby's doctor must be advised of the situation, and the baby must be monitored for side effects. Discuss the situation with your OB/GYN and your pediatrician if medication is prescribed to you and you are breastfeeding.

Your Distress Can Affect Your Partner

If you experience baby blues or PPD, it can affect your partner. Prepare him for this situation before your baby is born. Explain to him that if it happens to you, it's only temporary.

There are some things you might suggest to your partner that he can do for himself, if you get blue or depressed.

- Tell him not to take the situation personally.
- Suggest he talk to friends, family members, other fathers or a professional.
- He should eat well, get enough rest and exercise.
- Ask him to be patient with you.
- Ask him to support you. He can provide his love and support to you during this difficult time.

WILL WE EVER HAVE SEX AGAIN?

Probably the last thing on your mind right now is resuming sexual relations. Many women express the feeling that sex at this time is too painful and too much to cope with. They need to rest, get enough sleep and get back into a routine before they start thinking about sex again.

Resuming sexual relations can be a little difficult. You may be concerned about pain. That's natural. The best thing you can do for yourself is to take it easy and go slowly. Don't have sexual intercourse until you feel ready. Share your feelings and concerns with your partner.

Your sex drive, and that of your partner, can be affected by stress, emotions and fatigue. In fact, there are physical reasons you may not feel like having sex, including your changing estrogen level, which can cause vaginal dryness and irritation. You are probably still bleeding, too. If you had an episiotomy, that may add to your discomfort. And with all the changes your body has gone through, you just may not feel sexy right now. That's OK.

In the past, we advised a woman to wait at least 6 weeks before having intercourse. Today, we tell a woman to let her body be her guide, but 6 weeks is still a good suggestion. You probably won't feel like it anyway until then. If you feel no pain or discomfort and your episiotomy is healed, you can resume sexual relations when you feel up to it. Be sure bleeding has stopped. For most women, this is at least 4 to 6 weeks after delivery. Talk to your partner to make sure he isn't expecting to resume relations with you 1 or 2 weeks after delivery when you're thinking it will be 4 to 6 weeks.

When you do decide to have sex again, you can take some steps to make the experience more enjoyable for both of you. Try the following.

- Be sure you are healed enough to have sexual intercourse. If you aren't sure, call your doctor for advice.
- Use lots of lubricant to relieve vaginal dryness and to avoid irritation from friction (avoid petroleum jelly if you use condoms).
- If you use the woman-on-top position, you can control the amount of penetration.
- Foreplay can add pleasure to your sexual experience.
- Don't focus on your body and the way it looks; if your partner says you're attractive, believe him.
- Remember, there are alternatives to sexual intercourse. Kissing and caressing can be great turn-ons.

When you decide to have intercourse, take precautions if you don't want to get pregnant again immediately. You can become pregnant *before* you have a menstrual period. Read the section on birth control that follows, and be sure to discuss birth-control options with your doctor.

··

FAST FACTS

If you used a diaphragm or cervical cap before pregnancy, you need to be refitted after the birth. The size of a woman's cervix often changes after she has a baby, so these devices might not fit correctly or work effectively after baby's birth.

··

BIRTH CONTROL AFTER PREGNANCY

Contraception after the birth of your baby can be important, so you probably want to consider all your options. Most women begin ovulating 6 to 8 weeks after birth if they are not breast-feeding. (Breastfeeding may delay ovulation and menstrual periods for a few months, but you ovulate *before* you have a period.) If you have unprotected sex when you ovulate, you could get pregnant again.

We know breastfeeding protects you against pregnancy to some degree, but breastfeeding is *not* an effective method of birth control by itself! If you breastfeed, it's important to consider birth-control methods if you don't want to get pregnant.

If you don't want to have another baby very soon, it's important to discuss birth-control options with your partner and your doctor in the hospital or at your 6-week postpartum checkup.

Contraception if You Breastfeed

Consider using some kind of contraception if you don't want a surprise pregnancy. There are many to choose from, even if you breastfeed. If you want to use a method that doesn't require seeing your doctor to get a prescription or require an in-office procedure, condoms and spermicidal foams and gels are available. However, these methods may not be as reliable as those prescribed by your doctor.

More-reliable contraception choices for a nursing mom include:

- diaphragms
- birth-control pills, called *minipills* (they contain the hormone progesterone and are safe for a nursing mom and her baby)
- Depo-Provera, a hormone injection given every 3 months
- an IUD (intrauterine device)
- once-a-month birth-control injection
- Norplant, small rods containing a hormone (progesterone) placed in the arm just under the skin

If you don't use some method of contraception while breastfeeding, you're living dangerously. Most women don't have periods while they are nursing during the first 6 months, but that is not always the case. And the longer you nurse, the greater the possibility you could ovulate and get pregnant. It's a mistake to think not having a period means you can't get pregnant!

Contraception if You Bottlefeed

Contraceptive choices for the bottlefeeding mom are the same as those listed above, with one exception. If you bottlefeed, use *regular* birth-control pills rather than the minipill.

Discuss your options with your physician while you are still in the hospital or at your 6-week postpartum visit. Make your selection after considering all your choices.

....

FAST FACTS

You can become pregnant again before you have a menstrual period. Most women begin ovulating 6 to 8 weeks after their baby is born, if they're not breast-feeding. When you have your first period, you have *already* ovulated!

....

PUTTING IT ALL IN PERSPECTIVE

The concerns we've discussed in this chapter are ones women face each day. Most of them are temporary and won't interfere much with life with your new baby. The key to dealing with something during your recovery period is to relax. Any of these situations is more easily dealt with if you don't add your own stress to it.

4

It's Time to Eat, Baby!

Feeding your baby is one of the most important things you do for him. The nutrition your child receives from you gives him the start in life he needs to grow and to develop through childhood into adulthood. It's also important for *you* to eat healthfully if you breastfeed.

You may have questions about what is right for you and your baby. Read this section dealing with breastfeeding and bottle-feeding. Talk to other mothers. The more information you have, the better able you are to make decisions about this important aspect of caring for your baby.

FEEDING A NEWBORN

When a baby is hungry, he exhibits definite signs of hunger, including fussing, putting his hands in his mouth and turning his head and opening his mouth when his cheek is touched. Most newborns eat every 3 to 4 hours; some feed as often as every 2 hours.

You may feed your baby at regular intervals to help him get on a schedule. Or you may decide to let your baby set his own schedule—some babies need to nurse more often than others. Sometimes a baby needs to feed more often than usual, especially during growth periods. A baby is usually the best judge of how much he needs at each feeding. Usually a baby will turn away from the nipple (mother or bottle) when he is full.

Some people may suggest you feed your baby water occasionally instead of breast milk or formula. Whether this is a good idea for your baby depends on many things, including your baby's weight, how well he is doing and whether he is hungry or thirsty. Talk to your baby's doctor before offering water.

· ·

FAST FACTS

Your doctor may suggest you continue taking your prenatal vitamin if you breastfeed. It contains extra iron and folic acid. Some women take prenatal vitamins throughout their baby's first year.

· ·

It's a good idea to burp your baby after each feeding; some babies need to be burped during a feeding. There are various ways to burp a baby, such as holding your baby over your shoulder or sitting him in your lap, and gently rubbing or patting his back. You may want to place a towel over your shoulder or at least have one handy in case he spits up. If your baby doesn't burp, don't try to force it.

Babies frequently spit up some breast milk or formula after a feeding. It's common in the early months because the muscle at the top of the stomach has not fully developed. When a baby spits up enough to propel the stomach contents several inches, it is called *vomiting*. If your baby vomits after a feeding, don't feed him again immediately. His stomach may be upset; it may be wise to wait until the next feeding.

FAST FACTS

Breast milk protects a baby from some infections; the incidence of ear infections is significantly reduced in babies who are breastfed longer than 4 months.

BREASTFEEDING OR BOTTLEFEEDING?

If you are able to breastfeed, it's usually the best way to feed baby. Breast milk contains every nutrient a baby needs. It's easily digested. Research shows breastfed babies have lower rates of infection because of the immunological content of breast milk. Breastfeeding provides the baby a sense of security and the mother a sense of self-esteem. However, if there are reasons you cannot or choose not to breastfeed, be assured that babies also do well on formula.

It won't harm your baby if you do not breastfeed. Don't feel guilty if you choose to bottlefeed your baby. Sometimes breastfeeding is not possible because of a physical condition or other problems. Sometimes a woman chooses not to breastfeed because of demands on her time, such as a job or other children to care for. An infant can get all the love, attention and nutrition he needs if breastfeeding is not possible.

FAST FACTS

More women choose to bottlefeed (about 2 to 1) than to breastfeed.

BOTTLEFEEDING AS ONE OPTION

Some women may feel they are not good mothers if they choose not to breastfeed. However, statistics show more women choose to bottlefeed than breastfeed their babies. We know your baby can receive good nutrition if you bottlefeed.

Bottlefeeding has many advantages that may be overlooked. Some women enjoy the freedom bottlefeeding provides. Others in the family can help care for the baby. A father can be more involved in caring for his child. Bottlefed babies are often able to go longer between feedings; formula is usually more slowly digested than breast milk. Bottlefeeding also lets you determine exactly how much your baby is taking in at each feeding. Bottlefed babies take from 2 to 3 ounces of formula at a feeding and usually feed every 3 to 4 hours for the first month.

You may have twins or triplets (or even more); these babies are often bottlefed because it can be more difficult and demanding to breastfeed multiples. If you have more than one baby, there are many ways you can provide your babies the nutrition they need. Also see the discussion that begins on page 62 on breastfeeding more than one baby.

....

FAST FACTS

Some women feel guilty if they do not breastfeed. However, only about 1 in 5 women breastfeeds beyond 4 weeks after birth.

....

When you bottlefeed, there are some tips to keep in mind to help make the experience healthy and happy for you and your baby.

- Wash your hands before you prepare formula.
- Thoroughly clean feeding equipment before use.
- Check formula expiration dates.
- If you prepare formula or bottles ahead of time, keep them refrigerated.
- Throw away all leftover formula.
- Get rid of bottle nipples that are hard or stiff.
- Once you find a formula baby likes, use it exclusively.

Research shows that feeding a baby with a slanted bottle is better. This design keeps the nipple full of milk, which means baby takes in less air. Swallowing air can cause discomfort to baby. A slanted bottle also helps ensure baby is sitting up to drink. When a baby drinks lying down, milk can pool in the eustachian tube and cause ear infections.

Bonding with a Bottlefed Baby

Some parents fear bottlefeeding will not encourage closeness with their child; they believe that bonding will not occur between parent and baby. There are many ways you can bond with your baby. Studies show that carrying your baby close to your body in a slinglike carrier helps the bonding process. It's great because dads can also bond this way with baby.

There are also ways you can bottlefeed a baby that can help develop a closer bond between parent and child. Try the following ideas:

- Snuggle your baby close to you during feeding.
- Make eye contact, and talk to him.
- Heat formula to body temperature by running the filled bottle under warm water. However, there's no evidence that feeding refrigerated formula without warming it will harm your baby.
- Remove the bottle during feeding to let baby rest. It usually takes 10 minutes or longer to finish feeding.
- Don't leave the baby alone with the bottle. Never prop up a bottle and leave the baby to suck on it.
- Never put a baby down to bed with a bottle.

Types of Formula for Bottlefeeding

There are many different types of formula you can choose to feed your baby. Most babies do very well on milk-based formula, but some need specialized formulas. Several types are available on the market today, including:

- milk-based, lactose-free formula for babies with lactose-intolerance feeding problems, such as fussiness, gas and diarrhea
- soy-based, lactose-free for babies with cow's-milk allergies or sensitivity to cow's milk
- hypoallergenic protein formula, which is easier to digest and lactose-free for babies with colic or other symptoms of milk-protein allergy

The American Academy of Pediatrics recommends a baby be fed iron-fortified formula for the first year of life. Iron-fortified formula maintains adequate iron intake.

BREASTFEEDING AS YOUR OTHER OPTION

Many women choose to breastfeed their babies. It's a healthy way to feed your baby, and it can help create a close bond between mother and child. You can usually begin breastfeeding your baby within an hour (or sooner) after birth. This provides your baby with *colostrum*, the first

milk your breasts produce. Colostrum helps boost baby's immune system. Breastfeeding also causes your pituitary gland to release oxytocin, the hormone that causes your uterus to contract to keep bleeding to a minimum.

Don't be discouraged if you experience difficulty when you first start breastfeeding. It takes some time to find out what works for you and your baby. Hold your baby so he can reach the breast easily while nursing. Hold him across your chest, or lie in bed. Your baby should take your nipple fully into his mouth, so his gums cover the areola. He can't suck effectively if your nipple is only slightly drawn into his mouth.

· ·

FAST FACTS

When you breastfeed, your body produces between 20 and 30 ounces of milk a day, so keep up your fluid intake. Drink a glass of water *every time* you sit down to nurse.

· ·

Breastfeeding More than One Baby

If you have more than one baby, you should be able to breastfeed them. You may find it more challenging, but many mothers have done it. You can pump your breasts and divide the breast milk between (or among) your babies, then supplement with formula. Or you may breastfeed your babies for a short while at every feeding, then feed them formula. You may try to breastfeed exclusively. Studies have shown that frequent nursing stimulates milk production. Talk with your physician and your pediatrician about what might work best for you and your babies.

Bonding with a Breastfed Baby

Breastfeeding is an excellent way to bond with your baby because of the physical closeness. However, there are also other ways you can bond with your baby. See the discussion on page 141.

....

FAST FACTS

A woman who breastfeeds may lose weight more quickly after the birth of her baby than a woman who bottlefeeds but eats fewer calories.

....

Benefits of Breastfeeding

There are many benefits to breastfeeding your baby. One is the presence of DHA in breast milk. DHA (docosahexaenoic acid) is the primary structural fatty acid that makes up the retina of the eye and the gray matter of the brain. During pregnancy, your baby receives this important substance through the placenta. After birth, your breast milk continues to supply your baby with DHA. Why is this important for your baby? Studies have shown that a baby with DHA in his diet may have a higher IQ and greater visual development than babies fed formula; formula does not contain DHA at this time.

Another benefit is that it's nearly impossible for a baby to become allergic to his mother's breast milk; breastfeeding may prevent milk allergies. This is important if there is a history of allergies in your family or your partner's family. The longer a baby breastfeeds, the less likely he is to be exposed to substances that could cause allergy problems.

FAST FACTS

Nursing your baby for the first 4 weeks provides the most protection for him and the most beneficial hormone release to help you recover after the birth.

Research shows breast milk contains many benefits. Listed below are some other important reasons to breastfeed your baby.

- Breast milk offers protection from infection. Breastfeeding may help prevent diarrhea in infants, and it may inhibit the growth of bacteria that cause urinary-tract infections.
- Baby's permanent teeth may come in straighter.
- The risk of breast cancer may be lower for women who were breastfed.
- Breastfeeding may lower the risk of baby developing juvenile diabetes, lymphoma and Crohn's disease later in life.
- Women who breastfeed may have an easier time losing weight after delivery.

FAST FACTS

Women who nurse their babies have a lower incidence of breast cancer.

Disadvantages to Breastfeeding

There are some disadvantages to breastfeeding. One is that breastfeeding ties a woman so completely to the baby; a woman must be available when her baby is hungry. Family members may feel left out unless they can feed baby expressed milk.

A mother who breastfeeds must pay careful attention to her diet, both for the nourishment she takes in and to avoid foods and substances that pass into her breast milk that may cause problems for baby. Most substances you eat or drink (or take orally, as medication) can pass to your baby in your breast milk. Spicy foods, chocolate and caffeine are some things your baby can react to when you ingest them. Be careful about what you eat and drink during breastfeeding.

FAST FACTS

With the milk *letdown reflex* (which means milk is flowing into the breast ducts), your nipples will drip milk when your baby—or any other baby you're around—cries. Be sure to wear breast pads!

Tips to Get Started

It's not always easy to get started breastfeeding, even though you probably think it ought to be the most natural thing in the world to do. (It is, but it still takes practice!) Below are some tips to keep in mind.

- Relax in a comfortable place before you start. Make it a peaceful experience.
- Make sure baby is comfortable. Be sure he's dry and warm.
- Help baby connect with your breast. Brush your nipple across his lips. When he opens his mouth, place the nipple and as

much of the areola in his mouth as you can. You should feel him pull the breast while sucking, with no pain.

- If you experience pain, disengage him by slipping your finger into the corner of his mouth and gently pulling down to break the suction.
- Don't rush—it takes time for your baby to nurse. It takes longer for a baby to nurse than to drink a bottle. It may take as long as 20 to 25 minutes.

How Breastfeeding Affects You

Take good care of yourself when you breastfeed. Keep your fluid intake up. Don't diet. All the nutrients your baby receives from breastfeeding depend on the quality and quantity of the food you eat. Breastfeeding makes even greater demands on your body than pregnancy. Your body burns up to 1,000 calories a day just to produce milk!

While breastfeeding, eat an extra 500 calories a day to ensure adequate caloric intake.

FAST FACTS

Eat healthfully during breastfeeding. Avoid junk food and empty-calorie foods. Eat protein, dairy products and complex carbohydrates, and drink lots of fluid.

Warning Signs in a Breastfeeding Mother

You need to take extra special care of yourself when you breastfeed. Below are signs that might indicate you have a problem. If you experience any of these problems, call your doctor immediately.

- fever or chills
- extreme fatigue and body aches, as if you have the flu
- burning pain in either or both breasts
- red streaks on the breast
- lumpy areas in your breasts
- feeling of warmth in either breast
- swollen breasts, which keep baby from latching on to the nipple
- sore, cracked or bleeding nipples
- milk that does not flow freely
- low milk supply
- any feelings of depression or extreme sadness

S O S

 If you don't think your baby is getting enough breast milk, call your pediatrician. He or she will be able to give you advice on what to look for to determine how much breast milk baby is taking in.

Warning Signs in Baby

Nursing will almost certainly settle into an enjoyable routine for you and your baby, and he'll probably grow and thrive on breast milk. Warning signs may also be seen in your baby. If you experience any of the following with your infant, call your pediatrician.

- Baby doesn't wake up or stay awake long enough to nurse.
- Baby is fussy after nursing and cannot be settled by feeding again.
- Baby wets fewer than six diapers a day.
- Baby has fewer than two bowel movements a day.
- Baby has signs of jaundice, such as a yellowish tinge to his skin or eyes.

....

FAST FACTS

The consistency of breast milk changes from thinner to richer as baby nurses. When you begin a new feeding, try to start your baby on the breast you nursed last.

....

Your Milk Production

Some women worry they won't have enough breast milk to feed their baby. This is not a common problem. With some practice and lots of patience, nearly every woman can breast-feed her baby. To have breast milk available so baby can drink it while you are away from him, you can "express" it. Do this by using a breast pump (hand, battery-powered or electrically operated) to remove milk from your breasts.

It takes time to express your milk—perhaps 10 to 30 minutes, depending on the type of pump you have. Electric pumps work best; they can be rented at many medical supply stores. You'll probably have to express your milk one to four times a day (around the time you would normally nurse). Find a comfortable, private place where you can relax enough for milk letdown to occur.

If you freeze breast milk, don't thaw it in the microwave. Radiation can destroy substances in the milk that help protect a baby from infection.

Storing Breast Milk

Store your breast milk after you express it. There are several steps to take to store breast milk safely.

- Pump or express milk into a clean container.
- Label the container with the date and amount of milk collected.
- Expressed milk can be refrigerated or frozen and saved. Milk doesn't need immediate refrigeration; it will stay fresh for up to 4 hours at temperatures as high as 77F (25C) and for up to 24 hours at 60F (15.5C). You can keep fresh breast milk at room temperature for a few hours; it's best to refrigerate it as soon as possible. Breast milk can be safely stored in the refrigerator for up to 72 hours.
- You can freeze breast milk. Keep it in a refrigerator freezer for 6 months or in a deep freezer (−20F; −29C) for up to 12 months. Fill the container only 3/4 full to allow for expansion during freezing. Freeze milk in small portions, such as 2 to 4 ounces (56 to 112g), because these amounts thaw more quickly.

You can combine fresh breast milk with frozen breast milk. First, cool fresh breast milk (that you have just expressed) before combining it with thawed milk. The amount of thawed breast milk must be more than the amount of fresh breast milk. Never refreeze breast milk!

There are ways to thaw breast milk so it maintains its high quality.

- Put the container of frozen milk in a bowl of warm water for 30 minutes, or hold the frozen container under warm running water.
- Do not microwave breast milk; it can alter its composition.
- Swirl the container to blend any fat that might have separated during thawing.
- Feed thawed milk immediately, or store in the refrigerator for up to 24 hours.

Don't bottlefeed your baby with formula, if you have a choice. Your milk supply is driven by your baby's demand. Breastfed babies eat about every 2 to 3 hours in the first few weeks of life. If you bottlefeed formula part of the time, your baby won't demand the breast milk from you, and your body will slow down its production.

....

FAST FACTS

Even if you get a breast infection during nursing, your milk will be OK. It won't harm your baby.

....

SOME COMMON PROBLEMS DURING BREASTFEEDING

Breast milk becomes more plentiful between 2 and 6 days after birth, when it changes from colostrum to mature milk. Your breasts may become engorged and may cause you some pain for 24 to 36 hours. Continue breastfeeding during this time, even if your breasts are sore. Wear a bra that offers good support for your sore breasts, and apply cold compresses to your breasts for short periods. Take acetaminophen (Tylenol) if pain is severe, but don't take anything stronger, unless your physician prescribes it.

Soon after your baby begins to nurse, you will experience a tingling or cramping in your breasts, which means milk is flowing into the breast ducts. It occurs several times during feeding. Occasionally a baby will choke a bit when the milk comes too quickly.

Sore Nipples

Your nipples may become sore when you begin breastfeeding. If your baby doesn't take your nipple fully into his mouth during breastfeeding, his jaws can compress the nipple and make it sore. However, it's good to know sore nipples rarely last longer than a couple of days. Continue breastfeeding, even if nipples are sore.

There are other ways to help avoid sore nipples. Nipple shields, worn inside your bra between the nipple and bra fabric, provide some relief. They prevent tender skin from rubbing on the bra fabric. A mild cream can also be applied to sore nipples to provide some soothing relief. Ask your pharmacist or doctor to recommend products that are OK to use during nursing.

Breast Infections

You can get a breast infection, or *mastitis*, while you are breastfeeding. Large red streaks that extend up the breast toward the armpit, hard and painful lumps in the breast, fever or flulike symptoms usually indicate a breast infection. Call your doctor immediately; an infection can cause a fever to develop within 4 to 8 hours after the appearance of the red streaks. Prompt medical treatment can improve the symptoms and even clear up the infection within 24 hours.

Apply a warm compress to the affected area, or soak the breast in warm water. Express milk or breastfeed while massaging the tender area. If you develop flulike symptoms with a sore breast, call your doctor. Antibiotic treatment may be started. You may need to rest in bed; empty your infected breast by pumping or breastfeeding every hour or two. Left untreated, a breast infection can turn into an abscess. This is very painful and may need to be opened and drained.

There are several things you can do to help prevent a breast infection. Eat right, and get plenty of rest to keep your immune system working efficiently. Don't wear tight-fitting bras, especially underwire types, because they can block milk flow, which may cause an infection. Empty your breasts on a regular schedule to avoid engorgement. After each feeding or pumping, let nipples air-dry for a few minutes.

Don't stop nursing if you get a breast infection. If you stop, the infection may get worse. This occurs because you are still making milk. If you stop breastfeeding, breasts become more engorged and more painful.

Plugged Milk Ducts

Another situation you might encounter during breastfeeding is a *plugged milk duct*, which prevents milk from flowing freely. It results in areas of the breast that become more painful after breastfeeding. A plugged duct is not red, and you will not have a fever.

Treatment is usually unnecessary with a plugged duct. It usually takes care of itself if you continue to nurse frequently. Applying warm compresses to the sore area helps with the pain and may help open the duct. You can also take acetaminophen for the pain.

Colds and Viruses

If you have a cold or other virus, it's all right to continue breastfeeding. If you're taking an antibiotic, it's OK to breastfeed if the medication is compatible with nursing. Ask your doctor or pharmacist if any medication prescribed for you should be avoided while breastfeeding. Be sure to ask *before* you begin taking it.

S O S

 You may believe over-the-counter medications are OK, but call your pediatrician *before* you take any medication, especially if you're breastfeeding.

Medications You May Take

Be careful about taking any medications while you are breastfeeding. Although there are many situations in which medication is beneficial for you, sometimes it can have a negative effect on baby.

Take a medication *only* when you really need it. Ask your physician for the smallest dose possible. Check with your pharmacist, your OB-GYN and your pediatrician to see if it's OK to use a particular medication while breastfeeding. Ask about possible effects on the baby, so you'll be alert for them. Postpone treatment, if possible.

If you take a medication immediately after nursing, it may have less of an effect on the baby. If a medication could have serious effects on your baby, you may decide to bottlefeed for the time that you must take the medication. You can maintain your milk supply by pumping (then disposing of) your expressed milk.

Avoid Eating Peanuts

Research now indicates a woman should avoid eating peanuts and peanut products if she breastfeeds. If a child has a predisposition to a peanut allergy, exposure through breast milk as an infant could trigger the allergy, which can be very dangerous in some people. Peanut proteins pass into breast milk, and thus to the infant.

....

FAST FACTS

It's OK to have an occasional glass of wine or beer, just don't overdo it. You can treat yourself, even if you're breastfeeding. Drink the alcoholic beverage *immediately after* breastfeeding so your body has time to metabolize it before your baby nurses again. A small amount of alcohol passes out of the body within about 3 hours after consumption.

....

COMMON BREASTFEEDING SITUATIONS

Nursing in Public

Some women feel uncomfortable breastfeeding their baby in public. In many countries, breastfeeding in public is a natural part of life. If you feel uncomfortable nursing in a public place, go into the ladies' room or a lounge, and feed your baby there. Look at each instance by itself—you'll soon learn how comfortable you feel feeding your baby away from home.

Baby's Feeding Pattern

You may be unprepared for how often your baby will want (and need) to nurse in the first few weeks after birth. You may wonder if it's worth it to continue. Relax and be patient. It takes time for your baby to establish his nursing pattern. By the end of the second or third week, a pattern will probably become established, and your baby will sleep longer between feedings.

Avoid Bottles, when Possible

It's best to avoid bottles to supplement breastfeeding for the first month of breastfeeding for two reasons. Your baby may come to prefer feeding from a bottle (it's not as hard to suck), and your breasts may not produce enough milk.

How Long Should I Breastfeed?

Nursing the first 4 weeks of your baby's life provides the most protection for your baby and the most beneficial hormone release to help you recover after the birth. Nursing for the first 6 months is beneficial for your baby; it provides excellent nutrition and protection from illness.

After 6 months, the nutrition and protection aspects are not as critical for your baby. If you can nurse only a short period of time, that's OK. Try to stick with it for the first 6 months or at least for the first 4 weeks.

Breastfeeding at Work or While You're Away

It is possible to continue breastfeeding your baby after you return to work. If you breastfeed exclusively, you will have to pump your breasts or arrange to see your baby during the day. Or you can nurse your baby at home and provide formula when you're away.

You may find it necessary to be away from your baby for a few days during breastfeeding. If this is necessary, you will probably need to pump your breast milk while you are gone. If you don't, you may be very uncomfortable because breast milk will continue to come in. Take a breast pump with you, and discard the breast milk after it is pumped.

Clothes to Wear While Breastfeeding

It may be most comfortable to wear a nursing bra if you breastfeed. They have cups that open so you can breastfeed without having to get undressed. They also provide very good support for your enlarged breasts.

There are other special clothes you might want to consider wearing if you breastfeed. Many nightgowns, shift dresses and full-cut blouses have discreet breast openings so you don't have to get undressed to breastfeed. You can reach up inside your outer clothing, unhook your nursing bra and place your baby at your breast without anyone noticing. Lightly draping a towel or baby blanket over your shoulder and over the baby's head adds further coverage.

A nursing cape can also provide privacy. The cape is a large square of fabric, with a head-sized opening in the middle. The hole is placed over the mother's head, and the rest of the fabric covers the mother's chest and back, also covering the nursing baby. No blankets to slip off your shoulder!

If You Have a Chronic Illness

Some breastfeeding mothers have special medical problems they must deal with. If you have a chronic illness, you may need to make certain changes in your diet, medication use or daily activities. Discuss the situation with your doctor *before* making any changes.

Breastfeeding after Breast Surgery

Many women who have had breast-enlargement surgery are able to breastfeed successfully. Check with your doctor if you have silicone implants or if you are concerned about safety.

If you have had breast-reduction surgery, you should still be able to breastfeed. The surgery may result in decreased milk production, but usually there is enough milk to satisfy a growing baby.

Help from the Family

Your partner can still feel he is part of the family when you breastfeed. He can help out by getting up at night and bringing the baby to you or by changing the baby's diaper. Your partner can also feed your baby expressed breast milk. You can include other family members, such as older children, by letting them hold or burp the baby after he is fed. If you express your milk, an older child could feed the baby a bottle of it.

Switching Breasts during Breastfeeding

It's a good idea to switch breasts during breastfeeding, but wait until your baby finishes with one breast before switching to the other one. At the next feeding, start your baby on the breast you nursed last. This helps you keep both breasts stimulated. If your baby only wants to nurse from one breast each feeding, switch to the other breast the next feeding.

If You Need Help with Breastfeeding

If you experience problems, many hospitals have breastfeeding specialists who can help you. Personnel at your doctor's office may be able to refer you to someone knowledgeable. You can also look in the telephone book for the local La Leche League, an organization that promotes breastfeeding. Someone from the local group can give you advice and encouragement. Attending a La Leche meeting is also a good way to get to know other new mothers.

WEANING YOUR BABY

When you decide to discontinue nursing, you can either taper off gradually or stop cold turkey. Each way has its advantages. If you want to taper off gradually, offer a bottle at every other feeding or offer bottles during the day and nurse only at night. In the past, medication was given to stop milk production; however, these medications are no longer used. If you stop nursing suddenly, you may have some sleepless nights with a screaming baby, and you may be quite uncomfortable physically with engorged breasts. However, this method takes less time.

Some women like to nurse until they return to work. Others nurse through the first year. It depends on your situation and your desire, and when your baby gets teeth!

5

Eating Right to Get Back in Shape

After a woman gives birth, often one of her first concerns may be regaining her prepregnancy figure. Some women mistakenly believe they can get in shape and look better faster if they go on a "crash" diet, cutting calories to lose the weight they gained during pregnancy. While this may seem like a good idea, it really isn't. Your body needs time to recover from the grueling 9-month experience that has just ended.

Weight gain during pregnancy is normal and expected. Even if you don't breastfeed, your body adds extra fat to prepare for this important event. Nature also knows that a new mother needs extra energy, and the fat the body gains during pregnancy prepares her for the many demands of motherhood. Cutting calories isn't going to help your body meet these demands.

Eat nutritiously, develop and follow an exercise program, and realize it's going to take time! A discussion of some nutrition tips that can help you begins on page 82.

GETTING BACK IN SHAPE

Two important facts about getting in shape after pregnancy.

1. It took 9 months for your body to change. Accept the fact it will take some time to get back in shape.

2. You need to exercise to get your body back in shape.

Food Choices to Help You Get Back in Shape

- Do not crash diet—even if you're bottlefeeding your baby. Your body needs a balanced diet for energy.

- Drink plenty of fluids, especially water.

- Avoid junk food and empty calorie foods. Eat protein, complex carbohydrates and dairy products.

- If you are breastfeeding, you may need to eat as many as 500 extra calories a day to produce breast milk.

Exercising Know-How

- Talk to your doctor *before* you start an exercise program. If you had a C-section or birth complications, you may need to take special precautions.

- Be smart about exercise. Don't push yourself too much.

- Do an activity you enjoy that you'll stick with.

- Begin with light exercise and gradually work into a more strenuous program.

- Do Kegel exercises to increase strength of vaginal walls and the vaginal floor (see Chapter 6, page 100). Kegels help with incontinence, too.

- Don't compare yourself with anyone else—even your prepregnancy self.

- Understand (and try to accept) the fact that your body may have changed permanently because of the pregnancy.

- Exercise can help with postpartum distress (baby blues).

- Work out with another new mom. It's good emotional support because you both probably tire easily, you've both experienced body changes, neither of you has any time to waste and you can encourage each other.

- If you begin to get bored exercising, make changes. Try a new routine. Work out in a different place or at a different time.

- Wear the right clothes and shoes. A sports bra may be very beneficial for sore breasts.

SOS

Call your doctor if you are having problems with your nutrition plan. You need to eat well, but you probably want to lose weight, too. If weight doesn't seem to be coming off with exercise and healthy eating, you may need to see a nutritionist.

GETTING BACK IN SHAPE

Follow a nutritious eating plan, such as the one you followed during pregnancy. Continue to eat foods high in complex carbohydrates, such as grain products, fruits and vegetables. Lean meats, chicken and fish are good sources of protein. For your dairy products, choose low-fat or skim types.

Eat a variety of foods to provide the nutrients you need. Eat these foods in a form as close to their natural state as possible. You don't have to eat three big meals a day; you may prefer to spread food out over five or six small meals. Eating many small meals helps keep your energy levels stable. Another suggestion is to eat a combination of protein, carbohydrates and a little bit of fat each time you eat. This helps keep your blood sugar level up.

If you bottlefeed your baby, you need fewer calories than you would if you were breastfeeding. Don't drastically cut your caloric intake in the hopes of losing weight quickly. You still need to eat nutritiously to maintain good energy levels. Be sure the calories you eat are not from junk foods.

We've included information on the types and quantities of foods to eat every day for bottlefeeding mothers and those who choose to breastfeed. See pages 88 and 90 for examples of daily

menus. Choose 9 servings from the bread/cereal/pasta/rice group, if you breastfeed, and 6 servings, if you bottlefeed. Servings of fruit should be 4 for breastfeeding women, 3 for mothers who bottlefeed. Eat 5 servings of vegetables if you nurse, and 3 servings if you don't. Eat 3 servings from the dairy group while breastfeeding, and 2 servings if you don't. The amount of protein in your diet should be 8 ounces for a breastfeeding woman, and 6 ounces for a bottlefeeding woman. Be particularly careful with fats, oils and sugars; limit intake to 4 teaspoons for nursing mothers, and 3 teaspoons for nonnursing mothers.

During breastfeeding, keep your fluid intake high. Your body produces 20 to 30 ounces of milk each day, so your fluid intake is very important. Your body will get the fluid somewhere; if you don't drink extra fluids, you could become dehydrated. Drink plenty of water or other beverages to help you meet this goal, but avoid beverages that are high in calories, such as sodas.

NUTRITION PLAN FOR
BREASTFEEDING MOTHERS

Breastfeeding can be good for you, as well as for your baby. Making breast milk is a strenuous job; your body may respond by burning more calories, which may help you lose weight faster. As during pregnancy, you may be eating for two, but you don't have to eat twice as much!

A well-balanced diet during breastfeeding helps you maintain energy levels and good physical health. Your doctor may recommend that you continue your prenatal vitamins if you breast-feed. They contain iron and folic acid. Your body can use the extra nutrients during this important time. Some women take them throughout their baby's first year.

....

FAST FACTS

Be careful with your caffeine intake. It can have a greater effect on baby than you might believe.

....

You may also need supplemental iron, especially if you lost a lot of blood at delivery. Ask your doctor about it before you leave the hospital. Even if you don't need extra iron, it's a good idea to eat foods rich in the mineral for your continued good health. Foods rich in iron include meats, liver, dark-green leafy vegetables, such as spinach, kale and chard, dried beans, dried fruits and whole-grain products.

Other vitamins and minerals you need include calcium, zinc, magnesium, folic acid, vitamin B_6 and vitamin D. Calcium is necessary for your bone strength. You can get calcium from dairy products (choose those low in fat calories, if necessary) and calcium-fortified food products, such as orange juice. Zinc, which is important for wound healing and a healthy immune system, can be found in some seafood, beef and the dark meat of chicken or turkey. Magnesium is essential for muscles and bones; good sources include bran cereal, spinach, lentils, white potatoes and winter squash.

Folic acid, now added to many foods in the United States, is necessary for healthy blood cells. Lentils, spinach, broccoli, orange juice and various beans are excellent sources. Vitamin B_6 helps your body metabolize foods and helps maintain central nervous system function. Chicken, fish, pork and some types of beans are good sources. Vitamin D is a must for proper calcium absorption. Milk is the best source.

....

FAST FACTS

A breastfeeding mother's diet may affect whether a baby has colic. If your baby has problems with foods you eat, avoid them for a while. As the baby's digestive system matures, you might want to try them again.

....

FOODS TO AVOID DURING BREASTFEEDING

You've probably heard that some foods that you eat may cause problems for your baby. This is true. It's also true that some other substances you ingest, such as medications, may cause problems for your nursing infant. It's a good idea to think along the lines that "anything I eat may pass into my breast milk, and thus to my nursing baby." If you're unsure whether you should eat something or take a particular substance, especially medicine of some kind, call your doctor before you take it.

Many women ask about caffeine and alcohol. We know that both of these substances pass into your breast milk, so use caution when you eat foods or drink beverages that contain them.

Caffeine

Caffeine passes into your breast milk but only in small amounts. If you take in moderate amounts, such as drinking two or three cups of coffee a day, it probably won't affect your baby. If you notice fussiness or wakefulness in your baby, gradually cut back on your caffeine intake to see if it makes a difference.

Alcohol

It's OK to have an occasional alcoholic beverage while breast-feeding, if you limit your intake. Alcohol passes into breast milk very quickly; it passes out very quickly, too.

Too much alcohol can affect your baby and your milk production. It can make your baby very lethargic, and it can inhibit your milk production.

Chocolate and Other Foods

You may have heard from some people that various foods you eat, such as chocolate or spicy foods, can affect a nursing baby. This may be true; it all depends on the mother and the baby. Some babies are not bothered by the various foods the mother eats. Others have gas or become fussy if the mother ingests certain foods. You may have to experiment and see what happens.

If you find your baby extremely fussy after you eat Mexican food or Indian food, for example, avoid it until after you wean your baby. Or wait until some time has passed to try it again. Avoid peanuts and peanut products. See the discussion in Chapter 4.

Can Colic Result from Foods You Eat?

Studies have shown that a breastfeeding mother's diet may affect whether the baby has colic. (See the discussion that begins on page 128 for more information on colic.) Although the causes of colic are unknown at this time, certain foods have long been suspected of contributing to the problem.

Various studies have had nursing women keep a record of their diet and corresponding fussiness in their babies. When women ate cauliflower, cabbage, broccoli, cow's milk, onions and chocolate, their babies were more colicky.

At this time, we don't recommend avoiding any foods to prevent colic, but we suggest you be aware if foods cause problems for your baby. The foods listed above may be ones to limit or to avoid during breastfeeding, if your baby has problems after you eat any of them.

Baby's Allergies to Some Foods

Some babies react to a particular food in the mother's diet. The most common problem-causing foods are cow's milk and other dairy products. If you suspect your baby may be allergic to the dairy products you consume, eliminate them from your diet for a couple of weeks. It can take quite awhile for symptoms to improve.

If you must cut out an important food from your eating plan, such as dairy products, consult a nutritionist for guidance. Your doctor can also help you with this situation. The food that you must eliminate might be very important for you, but there should be ways to compensate with other foods.

MENUS FOR BOTTLEFEEDING AND BREASTFEEDING MOMS

Below are sample menus for both bottlefeeding and breastfeeding moms. Each day's plan contains a selection of nutritious foods from the food groups you need during this important time. The quantity of food in these sample plans is for a woman who weighed 130 pounds before pregnancy.

If You Bottlefeed

A day's nutrition for a bottlefeeding mother is different from that of a woman who breastfeeds. You don't need to consume as many calories, and your fluid intake doesn't need to be as high.

Breakfast
1/2 toasted English muffin
1 T. peanut butter
4 ounces plain yogurt

Midmorning Snack
1/2 cup peaches, fresh or canned in water
4 ounces skim milk
1 cereal bar

Lunch
2 cups salad
2 T. light salad dressing
2 slices bread
1 slice low-fat cheese
1 piece of fruit, such as an apple or pear

Midafternoon Snack
1 slice of toast
4 ounces skim milk
1 small piece of fruit

Dinner
1 small chicken breast
1/2 cup sautéed fresh vegetables
1 slice whole-wheat bread
sliced tomatoes
1 glass water

Snack
1 cup instant fat-free cocoa
1 small cookie

If You Breastfeed

Nutrition for a nursing mother needs to be high quality, but it should taste good, too! The foods listed on page 90 supply you with the nutrition you need to help you make breast milk and to give you energy.

Breakfast
1 egg, scrambled or poached
2 slices toast
1 T. margarine
1/2 grapefruit or cantaloupe
8 ounces skim milk

Midmorning Snack
1 cup tea
1 cup grapes
2 crackers

Lunch
2 cups salad
2 T. light salad dressing
2 slices bread
1 slice low-fat cheese
1 piece of fruit, such as an apple or a pear
8 ounces of water

Midafternoon Snack
1 slice of raisin toast
1 T. margarine
1/2 cup low-fat cottage cheese
1/2 cup fruit

Dinner
1 small chicken breast
1-1/2 cups sautéed fresh vegetables
2/3 cup brown rice
sliced tomatoes
8 ounces of water

Snack
4 ounces plain yogurt
4 small crackers

6

Exercising Your Way Back to Fitness

One of the most frequently asked questions after a baby is born is, "How soon can I start exercising?" After months of watching their bodies change so dramatically, many women want to get back in shape as soon as possible. They want to get their bodies back in shape and are eager to begin exercising soon after their baby is born. Exercise can be very important to help you feel better and to lift your spirits. It can also increase your circulation, help you heal and ease body soreness. There are many things you can do to get back in shape.

Begin by doing simple isometric exercises immediately after delivery. Practice holding your stomach muscles in. When you go to the bathroom, tighten your pelvic-floor muscles and abdominal muscles; start and stop your urine stream for a good workout. Even sitting down can be an exercise—sit tall in a chair while tightening pelvic-floor muscles and abdominals. Plant feet firmly on the floor.

Align hips and shoulders while sitting straight in your chair. Open your shoulders, and lengthen your neck. Keep head high.

···

FAST FACTS

Don't believe the pictures and stories about women who can wear their prepregnancy clothes when they leave the hospital. It doesn't really happen!

···

When you are up and about in the hospital, you can do other forms of exercise, if you didn't have any complications during the pregnancy or birth that would prevent you from being active. When you feel able, get up and walk around in the hospital. Do mild stretching of your legs and arms, which may feel very good after delivery. During labor and delivery, you used many muscles and tensed them during pushing; stretching after recovery can relieve some tension and loosen your muscles.

Other exercises you can do include leg stretches, neck and shoulder rolls, shoulder shrugs, and foot and ankle circles. Ask your doctor or the nursing staff if it's OK to do these activities. You may begin a simple stretching program soon after you are up and about, if there are no contraindications. If you have done yoga exercises in the past, some of the gentler stretches may be good to do at this time.

Exercise is important to your feeling of well-being. If you exercised regularly during pregnancy, you may be able to continue with many of the same exercises. Your body is probably still in good condition, so after delivery you can begin exercising and increase your levels a little more quickly. One caution—don't expect to leave the hospital in the shape or physical condition you were in before you became pregnant. Let your body and your doctor be your guide as to how much you can do and how much intensity you can put into your exercising. Changes in your cardiovascular system caused by pregnancy can last up to 6 weeks postpartum, which can affect your ability to exercise.

Be positive. Many athletes have found their level of conditioning was better after pregnancy and delivery. There is hope!

Check with your doctor about any plans you have for exercising. He or she may have specific advice for you. After you have your doctor's go-ahead, start slowly and pay attention to how your body feels. Don't push it—you have plenty of time to build up your strength.

EXERCISING AFTER A C-SECTION

If you had a Cesarean delivery, exercise is very important. In the hospital, you'll probably be asked to cough and to take deep breaths to keep your lungs clear. Wiggle your toes to aid circulation. Walking may not be easy at first, but it helps minimize the

FAST FACTS

If you can do an exercise on a regular basis, no matter what the weather is or what kind of interruptions you may experience, you will be more successful in achieving your goal of fitness.

chances of developing blood clots. Check with your doctor before starting any regular exercise routine or exercise program.

It may take longer to get your stomach area back in shape than if you had a vaginal delivery. You may have to wait until after your 6-week checkup before you can do stomach exercises or crunches. Within 4 weeks, you should be able to get back into a regular exercise program. It might take longer, however, before you can engage in activities that require all-out effort, such as running or lifting heavy weights. Full recovery could take months.

If you experience any pain, significant increase in bleeding or other complications, listen to your body. These problems can be an indication that you are not fully recovered, so you may need to ease up on the level or intensity of your exercise.

S O S

 If your pulse rate exceeds 140 beats a minute during or after exercise, or if you feel dizzy, check with your doctor.

EXERCISING AT HOME

After you return home, choose a type of exercise that you enjoy, and do it on a regular basis. You may find that as much as you want to exercise, it's very difficult to fit it into your busy schedule. Try to allow time for it; do some type of aerobic activity for at least 20 to 30 minutes at least 3 times a week (5 times a week is best for getting back in shape).

Walking and swimming are excellent exercises to help you get back in shape. Some nonweightbearing activities are excellent, such as riding a stationary bicycle or working out on a stair stepper. Even mildly aerobic exercises, such as light step aerobics or water aerobics, can be started soon after delivery. If you want to do water exercises, your doctor will probably advise you to wait until bleeding stops completely, which could take from 3 to 6 weeks.

You might want to begin strengthening exercises, using light weights, very soon after your baby's birth. Use 1- or 2-pound weights for arm and leg exercises (use ankle weights for your legs).

Be careful about beginning an exercise program too soon. Don't overtire yourself; get adequate rest. Getting back into shape takes time. It's easy to feel discouraged when you begin because you probably want immediate results. As the saying goes, "It took 9 months for your body to get into the shape it is now." It'll take some time to get it back into the shape you would like to be in.

Don't be too hard on yourself, and don't expect miracles. It may take some planning and dedication on your part to fit an exercise routine into a busy, hectic schedule, but you'll be happy you did when you see positive results. And you'll find you have more energy, which you probably need now that you have a new baby to take care of!

* *

FAST FACTS

When you exercise, let your recovering body be your guide as to how much you can do and the level of intensity you put into your workout. Changes in your cardiovascular system from pregnancy can last for a while, which can affect your ability to exercise.

* *

ENSURING YOUR SUCCESS

There are some things you can to do to help yourself be success-ful in your workouts. To lose fat, do some type of aerobic activ-ity, such as biking, running, swimming or aerobic-exercise classes. These exercises use large muscle groups, elevate your heart rate and burn calories, which in turn burns fat your body stored during pregnancy. If you can work out 20 to 40 minutes 3 to 5 times a week, you'll find your body will respond fairly quickly.

You may feel self-conscious about exercising with others, if you feel out of shape. Find a class for new mothers, or exercise with someone else who has just had a baby. Work out when traf-fic is light at the gym, such as late morning or early afternoon.

If you can't get out to exercise, an exercise videotape you can buy, rent or check out from the library is another option. There are many on the market specifically for new moms. Or check out exercise programs on TV. You can work out while baby sleeps or your other children nap.

....

FAST FACTS

While trying to get back into an exercise routine, relax. It may take longer to lose weight; you may also find your body shape has changed due to pregnancy.

....

TIPS FOR STARTING
YOUR EXERCISE PROGRAM

You might want to consider the ideas on pages 97 and 98 as you plan your exercise program.

- Before you do anything, be sure to check with your doctor about starting an exercise program. If you had a Cesarean delivery, it's important to know that your body has healed and you are ready to exercise.

- Do something you enjoy. Choose some sort of exercise that you will continue on a regular basis. If you hate running, it's probably not a good idea to choose this form of exercise as your aerobic activity.

- Time may be limited, so use it wisely. If you have the chance to do something while your baby sleeps, do it.

- Work out when you can. Two or three 10-minute exercise sessions spread out during the day may be easier to handle than a full 20 or 30 minutes at one time.

- Pay attention to your nutritional needs. Don't go on a strict diet in an attempt to lose weight quickly. You need adequate nutrition to make breast milk, if you breastfeed. Even if you don't breastfeed, your body needs energy to take care of your baby and yourself, so don't skimp on your food. Eat nutritiously.

- Your body has undergone some major changes, so don't be too hard on yourself. It may take longer to lose weight, and you may find your body shape has changed because of the pregnancy. You may have to accept these changes because there may not be much you can do about them. Avoid the scale and weighing yourself. Instead, let your clothes be your guide. Tune in to your body, and check out how you feel. Use these measures as a gauge to determine your progress.

- Work out with a friend, especially another new mom. Walk together or agree to do some other type of activity. Take your babies when possible. If you know someone else depends on you for support, it may be easier to stay committed.

- If you find you're getting bored with your routine or you feel very tired, try to make some positive changes. Try another activity. Keep at it, even when you feel exhausted—sometimes exercise can help increase your energy level and make you feel less tired.

- Always warm up and cool down, whether you are doing aerobic activity or toning exercises. Warm up by walking briskly or marching in place for 5 to 10 minutes. When finished with your activities, cool down by stretching for at least 5 minutes.
- Drink lots of water. Start before you exercise, and keep hydrated all during your exercise session.

Before you begin exercising, you'll probably need to gather together some things to help make your workout easier and more enjoyable. Paying attention to these details before you begin will increase the enjoyment and benefits you receive from your exercise program.

- Wear the right clothes. Clothes should be comfortable and allow your body to "breathe."
- Wear shoes that offer good support.
- A sports bra, for your enlarged breasts, may provide added relief to sore breasts.

FAST FACTS

Abdominal skin cannot be strengthened, tightened up or made smoother by exercise. Exercise helps strengthen underlying muscles, but it won't give you back your prepregnancy figure. That depends on the connective tissue over your abdomen, the elasticity of your skin and how much body fat you retain.

EXERCISES TO TONE YOUR BODY

In this section, you will find a collection of various isometric and isotonic exercises that can help you get back in shape. *Isometric* exercises pit one muscle or part of the body against another or against an immovable object, such as a wall, in a strong, motionless action. These activities include pressing, pulling or pushing. *Isotonic* exercises tense the muscles against a heavy or resistant force; they help build muscle strength. These activities include weight lifting.

Exercises in this section are isometric and isotonic to help you build or regain strength in your muscles. Aerobic exercise should be pursued in addition to these activities because aerobic exercise increases the body's metabolism and helps burn fat.

Choose exercises from this section that focus on body areas you need to work on. Try to do these activities at least 3 times a week—every other day helps tone muscles. You might want to alternate aerobic activity and toning exercises from one day to the next.

You may notice that many of these exercises are for toning tummy muscles. We know this is an area many new mothers are very concerned about, so we have included quite a few for you to choose from.

Kegel Exercise

This exercise is one of the best ones you can do to help tighten pelvic-floor muscles; it's helpful in getting vaginal muscles in shape after delivery of your baby. You can do it anywhere, anytime. Tighten then release lower-pelvis muscles. Tighten muscles higher in the pelvis until you reach those at the top. Hold for a count of 10, then release slowly. Repeat 3 or 4 times. Good for toning pelvic-floor muscles.

Your Other Pelvic-Floor Strengthener

Lie on floor on your back. Place arms straight out from your sides. Cross one leg over the opposite ankle, and squeeze legs together. Hold 4 seconds, then release. Repeat with legs crossed the opposite way. Do 6 times for each side. Good for toning pelvic-floor muscles.

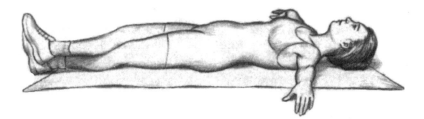

Leg and Back Stretch

Place a chair in the corner so it won't slide when you push against it. Place left foot on the chair seat; support yourself against the wall with your hand, if necessary. Stretch left leg behind you, lift chest and arch back. Turn shoulders and lean torso to left. Hold 25 to 30 seconds. Do 3 stretches for each side. Do this stretch before beginning abdominal exercises. Good for toning legs and back muscles.

Tummy Tightener

Lie on the floor. Lift both feet about 18 inches off the floor, bending knees at a right angle. Place hands under hips to support lower back. Raise head slightly, keeping shoulders and upper back on floor. Bring knees toward face while lifting your feet. Use abdominal muscles to lift legs; don't push against the floor with arms. Hold for a count of 5. Begin by doing 3, and work up to 25. Good for toning tummy muscles.

Lower-Belly Tightener

Lie on back on floor, with hands at sides. Holding feet together, cross ankles, bend knees and lift legs up to a 90-degree angle. Using lower abdominals, not pushing with your hands, lift hips a few inches, hold then release. Work up to 15 repetitions each day. Good for toning tummy muscles.

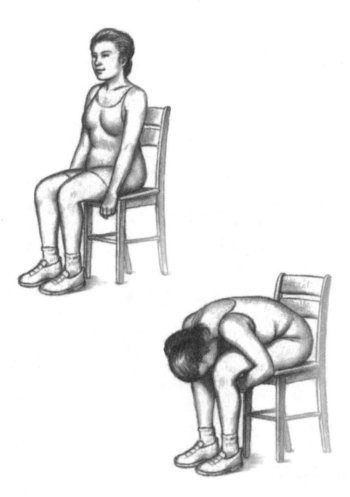

Stretch for Relief

To ease a tense back, sit on the edge of a chair, with knees 6 inches apart and feet facing front. Lean forward until your tummy touches your thighs. Clasp wrists together under your thighs. Breathe deeply through your nose, and let your chin drop onto your chest. Hold for 30 seconds, then push back to upright sitting position. Repeat 3 or 4 times. Good for easing tight back muscles.

Arm and Shoulder Stretch

Sit up straight. Lace fingers together behind your head; keep elbows apart. Inhale and push interlaced hands, with fingers still together, toward ceiling. Exhale and return hands to position behind your head. Repeat 5 times. Good for toning arms and shoulder muscles.

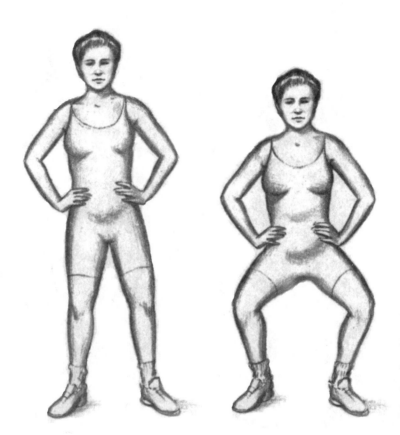

Leg Stretch

Stand with feet wider than shoulder width apart. Turn toes out slightly. Place hands on abdomen, and squat with knees over toes. Hold for count of 3. Keeping back straight, slowly raise to standing position. Repeat 8 times. Good for toning leg muscles.

Reverse Curls (also called Pelvic Tilts)

Lie flat on back, with knees drawn up so feet are flat on the floor. Place hands by your sides, keeping shoulders on floor. Squeezing buttock muscles together, lift hips from floor high enough so that you create a straight line between hips, knees and shoulders. Hold for count of 5, then slowly return hips to floor. Repeat 5 times. Good for tummy muscles.

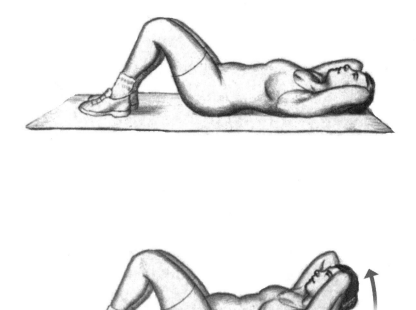

Tummy Crunches

Lying on the floor, bend knees and place feet flat on the floor. Place hands behind your head. Tighten tummy muscles as you lift head and shoulders slightly. Keep chin open (look forward and up). Hold crunch for 4 seconds. Repeat 5 times. Good for toning tummy muscles.

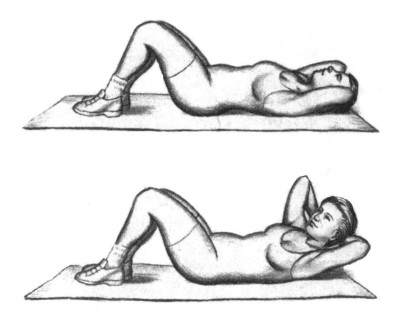

Side Crunches

To work the sides of your abdomen, position yourself as for the basic tummy crunch (above). When you lift, rotate toward one knee. Hold crunch for 4 seconds, then repeat for other side. Repeat 5 times. Good for tightening oblique muscles, which are on the sides of your waist.

Tummy Compressions

Like Kegel exercises, you can do this just about anywhere. Standing or sitting, take a deep breath and inhale. While exhaling, tighten tummy muscles as though you were zipping up a pair of tight jeans. Repeat 6 or 8 times. Good for toning tummy muscles.

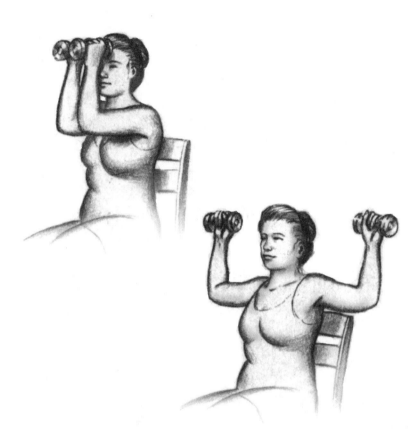

Breast Boosters

Sit on the edge of a chair. Using light weights (2 to 3 pounds each, to start), raise arms to shoulder level, and bend elbows to point hands toward ceiling. Slowly bring elbows and arms together in front of your face. Hold for 4 seconds, then slowly open to shoulder width. Repeat 8 times; work up to 20 times. Good for tightening breasts muscles, to keep breasts from sagging.

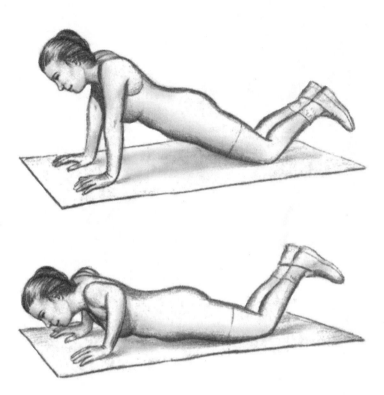

Pushups

Kneel on floor with weight on hands and knees. Bending elbows, lower chest toward floor while inhaling until you are
about 2 inches from the floor. Hold for a count of 2.
Straighten arms and push back up while exhaling. Hold for a
count of 3. Repeat 6 times. Good for strengthening arms and
back muscles.

Waist Toner

Stand with feet apart and knees relaxed. Holding a light weight in your right hand (a 16-ounce can will do fine), extend right arm straight over your head. Contract tummy muscles, bend slightly at the waist then swing arm down and over your left foot. Complete exercise by returning arm to original position, above your right shoulder. Repeat 8 times on each side. Good for slimming waistline.

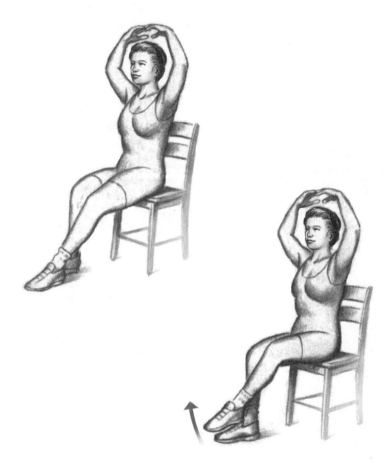

Leg Lifts

Sit on edge of chair, and place both feet flat on floor. Relax shoulders and curve arms over head. Keeping back straight, hold in abdominal muscles while you extend one leg out in front. Using thigh muscles only, lift leg about 10 inches off the floor. Hold for a count of 5, then slowly lower foot. Repeat 10 times with each leg. Good for toning thigh muscles, hips and buttocks.

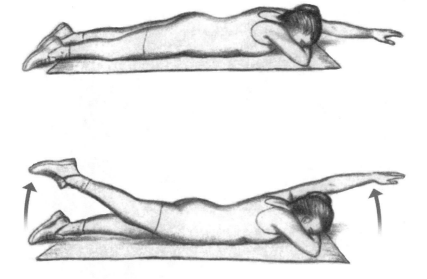

Spinal Extensions

Lie on your tummy with right hand under your forehead.
Stretch left hand in front. Together, slowly lift left hand and
right leg off floor. Hold for count of 2, then lower slowly. Repeat
8 times for each side. Good for strengthening back muscles and
toning tummy muscles.

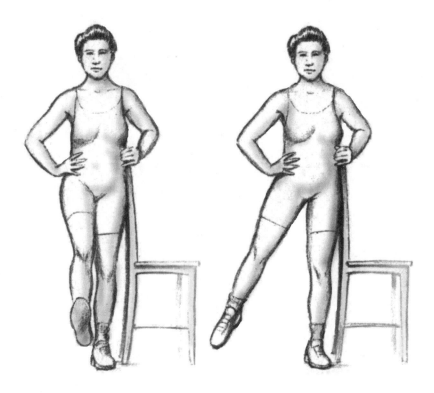

Side Leg Lifts

Hold onto door jamb or back of sturdy chair. Beginning with left leg, point your toe and lift leg forward to 90 degrees, then lower to floor. Without stopping, lift same leg to side, as far as you can but not beyond 90 degrees. Return to starting position. Repeat 10 times for each leg. Good for toning leg muscles and buttocks.

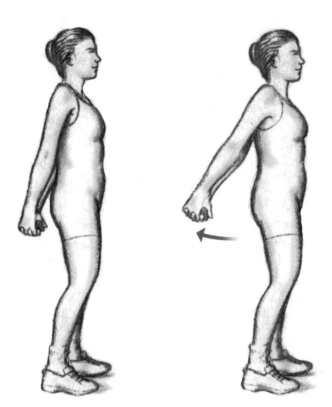

Upper-Chest Stretch

To help improve your posture, stand or sit on the floor, and clasp hands behind you. Lift arms until you feel a good stretch in your upper-chest area and upper arms. Hold for a count of 5, then lower arms. Repeat 8 times. Good for stretching arm muscles, back muscles and upper chest.

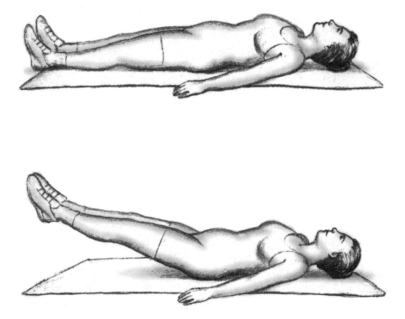

Double Leg Lifts

Lie on your back on the floor. Keeping both legs together, lift legs slowly from the hip. Be sure you use your tummy muscles for this one. Hold for 6 seconds, then slowly lower both legs to the floor. Work up to 8 repetitions. Good for toning tummy muscles.

7

Being a Family Is Fun!

You've looked forward for months to welcoming your new baby into your life. It's exciting to bond together and become a family. However, during your first days and weeks at home, you may begin to wonder if all your baby will ever do is eat, sleep and wet or mess in her pants. You may wonder if she will ever get on any type of schedule.

Let your baby develop her own schedule. You'll be able to make changes as your baby grows and develops. You may find your baby needs a lot of sleep. It's normal for a baby to get day and night mixed up for a while. Take heart—this doesn't usually last longer than a few weeks. If possible, keep baby awake and active during the day. It may help her get on a better sleep schedule.

In the first 4 weeks of life, your baby may sleep as many as 20 hours a day. You may wonder if she will ever be awake long enough for you to get to know her. She may only be awake long enough to feed, change and bathe her. Cuddle and bond during these times, too. Each day she will become more aware of you and her surroundings.

Babies eat quite often in the first few months of life, whether they are breastfed or bottlefed. A baby can eat every 2 to 4 hours. When your baby is quite young, feed her when she's hungry. Denying your baby food when she's hungry can cause her to become anxious. If you breastfeed, note each time you breastfeed and for how long. If you bottlefeed, note when your baby eats and how much she consumes. This is important information to share with your pediatrician on your baby's first visit.

....

FAST FACTS

You may need as many as 100 diapers a week for your newborn.

....

It's surprising to find out how often a baby needs to be changed! A baby wets her diaper every 2 to 4 hours; the number of bowel movements varies from one baby to the next. If you breastfeed, your baby may have a bowel movement only once every couple of days; this is normal. If you bottlefeed, your baby may have as many as six bowel movements a day, usually following a feeding. This, too, is normal. Change your baby's diaper as soon as possible. Babies have very delicate skin, and wet diapers can lead to diaper rash. If baby has diaper rash, a wet diaper can make it worse. And it hurts!

It's also normal for baby to cry. A baby cries to make her wants known—she has no other way of communicating with you. Some babies cry more than others. You'll soon learn to distinguish different cries in your baby. You'll be able to tell a "hungry cry" from a "lonely cry" or a "bored cry." It just takes time and practice. Until you learn what different cries mean, check the baby's diaper, burp her again and be sure she isn't uncomfortable. Sometimes your baby just wants to be held and loved by you.

S O S

 Babies cry! Plan ahead—decide whom you can call to talk to or to ask for help and support when your beautiful baby *won't stop crying!*

BEGINNING LIFE WITH YOUR BABY

Your baby is a precious creation—you must handle her with care. Your newborn lacks muscle control, so you'll need to take precautions to make sure you hold her correctly. It also helps to hold your baby in the correct positions because she tends to startle at sudden changes. Holding her correctly can avoid injury and yelps of fright. Try the following:

- Always keep your hand behind baby's head when you lift her or hold her at your shoulder.
- When carrying her in your arms, her head will probably extend beyond your elbow—be careful not to bump her head against the doorway or wall.
- Lift your baby slowly.
- Don't rush when you carry her.
- Don't move your baby too quickly.

Every parent has been overprotective with a new baby. You may dress your baby too warmly or keep her isolated from everyone else to avoid germs. You may check on her 10 times a night. It's OK to be cautious, but relax. Your baby needs to be exposed to people; you can't keep all infections away from her. It just isn't possible. It's probably best to avoid crowds, like those at malls or markets, for the first month, at least.

Keep your home temperature comfortable, and dress baby appropriately. It's unnecessary to keep your home "tropical." As a matter of fact, it could be detrimental for *everyone* in the family if you do this. Generally, 68F(20C) to 70F(21C) is a good range. Don't assume baby is cold just because her hands and feet are. The best indicator is your baby's mood. If you can't comfort your baby by holding or feeding her, she may be too hot or too cold.

When you do take your baby out, dress her appropriately. Keep her out of the wind and the sun, too. Layers work best— add one more layer than you have on or add a light blanket. Babies lose heat through their hands, feet and scalp, so be sure all three areas are well covered in cold weather.

While sunscreens can work wonders for you, don't use them on a baby younger than 6 months. They can be very irritating to delicate skin. Put a hat and protective clothing on baby for even a brief outing in the sun, especially in very hot, sunny areas.

You don't have to walk on tiptoes around your little one. It's just not practical. Usual household noises won't harm baby; being exposed to them will make her less sensitive to them. She'll have an easier time sleeping if she's used to the background noises of your home.

WHAT DOES YOUR BABY LOOK LIKE?

Your baby is born wet, usually with some blood on her body. A white or yellow waxy substance, called *vernix*, may cover part or much of her body. This is easily removed by cleaning the baby's skin.

You will probably notice that your baby's head is large in proportion to the rest of her body. It can look enormous on the baby's tiny body. At birth, the head measures 25% of her entire length. As she grows, this proportion will change until her head is only about 12% of her adult height. If your baby made her appearance into this world through the birth canal, her head may be misshapen or elongated. This shape is only temporary and becomes more normal appearing over the next few days.

You may notice other things about your baby's appearance that surprise you. Her cheeks may be pouchy, her eyelids swollen and her head pointy. A newborn's nose may look too flat to breathe through, but babies manage to breathe through them. These are normal and will change as she grows.

You may be distressed when you see the baby's pulse throbbing at the two soft spots on her head, called the *fontanels*. This is normal, so don't worry about it.

Your baby may be born with lots of hair or none at all. If she has an abundance of hair, it may fall out in the first 6 months; don't worry. The new hair may be entirely different in color and texture. If she's bald, it's not a permanent condition; her hair will eventually grow.

A newborn's eyes may be swollen or puffy immediately following birth because of the pressure in the birth canal. Swelling improves quickly. You may also notice your baby's eyes are slightly irritated and red. This is caused by the antibiotic ointment applied to her eyes shortly after birth to prevent eye infections. Irritation and redness usually disappear within a couple of hours.

One of your baby's eyes may wander when she looks at you, or she may look cross-eyed. Eye muscles aren't strong enough yet to control eye movements. A wandering eye usually corrects itself by the time the baby is 6 months old. If she still has a problem after that, discuss it with your pediatrician.

The skin folds at the inner corners of a baby's eyes may make it look as if the baby is squinting. As time passes, these folds become less prominent. Your baby's skin may be wrinkled, peeling, scratched, blotchy, hairy or pimpled, or it may look perfect. A newborn's skin often begins to dry out and may become flaky and scaly after birth. This condition can last for a few weeks. You don't need to treat it, but you may want to rub a little lotion into your baby's skin.

If you're worried that your baby may have been born with a disability or deformity, talk to your pediatrician about your concerns. This is all new to you, so it's OK to ask questions.

WHEN YOUR BABY CRIES

Most parents feel distress when they hear their baby cry—especially when they cannot comfort the baby. Crying is natural for babies; it's their way of communicating. When your baby cries, she is communicating to you that she is hungry, tired or lonely. Or she may be telling you she needs to be burped or changed. She might cry if she feels sick, scared or in pain. Sometimes a baby cries when she is overstimulated. After the first few weeks, you'll learn what her different cries mean.

The way you hold your baby brings special comfort to her. When you touch her, it tells her she is not alone. You won't spoil her if you comfort her when she's fussy. Finding the tricks that work with your baby usually comes through trial and error, but you'll eventually learn what works best for her. Some common solutions include reducing stimulation, giving the baby something to comfort her, such as her hand or a pacifier, wrapping her securely in a blanket, laying her on her stomach across your lap and stroking her, or softly humming or singing to her.

Occasionally a baby's crying can cause distress in you. If you find this happening, call a friend or relative to stay with baby so you can take a break. Get out of the house for a walk or some quiet time. Exercise helps relieve stress.

YOUR BABY'S HEALTH

It's inevitable—your baby will get sick sometime. Whether it's a cold, an ear infection, colic or something else, you need to be prepared. If your baby exhibits any of the following symptoms, call your doctor. Any of these could be an indication your baby is ill.

- fever higher than 101F (38.3C)
- inconsolable crying for long periods
- problems with urination
- projectile vomiting, in which stomach contents come out with great force
- baby appears lethargic or floppy when held
- severe diarrhea
- unusual behavior
- poor appetite

Dehydration

Dehydration in an infant can be very serious. If you think your baby may be dehydrated, call your pediatrician immediately. There are some warning signs to watch for, including those below.

- Baby wets fewer than five or six diapers a day.
- Baby's urine is dark yellow or orange; it should be pale yellow.
- Baby has fewer than two loose stools a day.

- Baby seems to be having trouble sucking.
- The soft spot on baby's head is sunken in.
- Baby is listless or otherwise appears unhealthy.

If you're concerned, call your doctor. A change in the number of diapers used or the consistency of the bowel movement is the first clue.

....

FAST FACTS

During pregnancy, your liver takes care of bilirubin for your baby. After delivery, if baby's liver isn't mature and can't handle the bilirubin, jaundice occurs.

....

Jaundice

Jaundice is a yellow discoloration of the skin, sclera (eyes) and deeper tissues of the body. The baby looks yellow because excess amounts of bilirubin, a breakdown product of blood, has accumulated in her system. The baby is unable to filter it from the blood. It can be dangerous for the baby if left untreated.

If your pediatrician and the nurses in the hospital suspect your baby has jaundice, they will test her and keep her under observation. They will determine what type of treatment is necessary.

Phototherapy is used to treat jaundice. The baby is placed under special lights, which penetrate baby's skin and convert the bilirubin to a form that is passed in the urine. In more severe cases, blood-exchange transfusions may be necessary.

In some parts of the world, special lights may not be available. In these cases, the baby is placed outside in the sunshine for very short periods of time, and the sunlight destroys the excess bilirubin.

Diarrhea

Your baby may experience diarrhea—it's not uncommon. She'll need extra water and minerals to prevent dehydration. Your doctor may recommend an electrolyte solution to help replenish your baby's lost fluids and minerals.

Ear Infections

It may be difficult for you to determine if your baby has an ear infection. Symptoms that may indicate an ear infection in babies less than 6 months of age include irritability that lasts all day, sleeplessness, lethargy and feeding difficulties. These symptoms may be hard to discern and may not be accompanied by fever.

For babies between 6 and 12 months of age, the symptoms are similar, except that fever is more common. The onset of ear

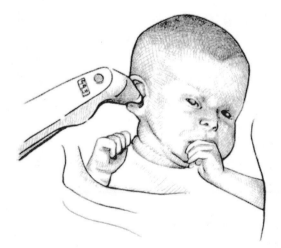

pain may be sudden, acute and more noticeable, and baby may pull at her ears. If you suspect baby has an ear infection, call your pediatrician. He or she can look into your baby's ears and will prescribe treatment.

Colic

Colic is a condition marked by episodes of loud, sudden crying and fussiness, which can often last for hours. About 20% of all babies experience this unexplained pain and crying. In full-blown colic, the baby's abdomen becomes distended, and the infant passes gas often. The only way to know if your baby has colic is to visit your pediatrician or family physician. He or she can determine if it is colic or if your baby is having some other problem.

Colic usually appears gradually in an infant about 2 weeks after birth. As time passes, the condition may worsen; however, it often disappears around age 3 months but occasionally lasts until 4 months. Colic attacks usually occur in the late afternoon and early evening, and can last as long as 3 to 4 hours. Attacks cease as quickly as they begin.

Researchers have been studying the causes of colic for a long time, but we still have little understanding of why it occurs. Theories about its causes include: immaturity of the digestive system, intolerance to cow's-milk protein in formula or breast milk, and fatigue in the infant.

At this time, we cannot offer a definitive answer on how to stop the colic. Most doctors recommend using a variety of methods to try to ease the baby's discomfort. Some of these ideas are:

- Offer baby the breast or a bottle of formula.
- Try noncow's milk formula, if you bottlefeed.

- Carry your baby in a sling during an attack. Motion and closeness often help somewhat.
- Give baby a pacifier to help soothe her.
- Put the baby on her stomach across your knees, and rub her back.
- Wrap the baby snugly in a blanket.
- Massage or stroke baby's tummy.

....

FAST FACTS

In the first 4 weeks of life, your baby may sleep as many as 20 hours every day. She may seldom be awake for longer than 25 to 30 minutes at a time.

....

YOUR BABY'S SLEEPING HABITS

Sleeping is very important for a baby; you'll soon realize what kind of sleep schedule is best for your infant. The wisest thing you can do as a parent is to establish a routine to help your baby develop healthy sleeping habits. The list below, continued on page 130, may give you some helpful hints to do this.

- Wait until your baby is tired to put her to bed.
- Develop a regular, predictable bedtime routine.
- Offer baby a pacifier or her thumb.
- Don't put your baby to bed with a bottle!
- Never leave your baby alone on a waterbed.
- Limit daytime naps to a few hours each.
- Don't overstimulate the baby when you get up for nighttime feedings.

- By day, let baby nap in a lighted area, with some noise. At night, put baby in a very quiet, dark room to sleep.
- Keep baby up during the day by talking and singing to her or providing other stimulation.
- Place baby on her side or back *every* time you put her to bed.

FAST FACTS

Sleep patterns may develop differently for bottlefed babies and breastfed babies. Bottlefed babies may sleep longer at night as they mature. Breastfed infants may not shift to longer sleep patterns until about the time they are weaned.

Place a baby on her side or back when putting her down to sleep. This position greatly reduces the incidence of SIDS (sudden infant death syndrome). Other safe sleeping tips include

making sure the mattress is safe and in good repair. Crib slats should be no farther apart than 2–3/8 inches. Don't use comforters, pillows or cushions that are soft, with loosely filled surfaces. They could interfere with baby's breathing. Avoid a waterbed crib mattress because it can trap baby and suffocate her.

Sleep patterns may develop differently for bottlefed and breastfed babies. Bottlefed babies often sleep longer at night as they mature. Breastfed infants don't usually shift to longer sleep patterns until they are weaned.

TAKING CARE OF BABY

You probably have other questions about how to care for your new baby. Some of these tips below may help.

- It isn't that difficult to deal with the stump of the umbilical cord. It will fall off 7 to 10 days after birth. Until it does, clean your baby with sponge baths.
- To remove sleepers from your baby's eyes, use a cotton ball moistened with clean water. Place the cotton ball at the inner corner of the eye, and wipe vertically down the nose.
- Never put anything into your baby's nose. If you need to remove dried nasal secretions, gently wipe around the nose. Dried nasal secretions are usually sneezed out.
- Never probe in your baby's ears with any object! Earwax is there for a purpose. It's OK to clean around the outside of the ears with a soft washcloth, but don't put anything inside your baby's ears.
- You will probably have to decide between cloth and disposable diapers. Your decision depends on your lifestyle, your budget and your baby. Disposable diapers are very convenient. You don't need pins or plastic pants, and you never have to wash

them. On the other hand, cloth diapers can be used many times. Some styles don't need pins or plastic pants. You will need adequate washing and drying facilities, or you may choose a diaper service. Many people use a combination of disposable and cloth diapers.

....

FAST FACTS

Keep your baby buckled up in a car seat every time you travel by car. One study showed that more than 30 deaths a year occur to unrestrained infants *going home from the hospital!*

....

CAR RESTRAINTS—
FOR THE SAFETY OF YOUR BABY

Every time your baby rides in the car, she should be restrained in an approved child safety-restraint seat. In an accident, an unrestrained child becomes a missilelike object in a car. The force of a crash can literally pull a child out of an adult's arms!

All states now have laws that govern safety-restraint systems. Call your local hospital or police department, and ask for information. Many hospitals won't let you take baby home if she is not going to ride in an approved safety-restraint seat. Many hospitals have loaner car seats you can borrow until you get your own.

The safest spot for baby in a car is in the middle of the back seat. In this position, baby is more protected in the event of a side collision. Manufacturers recommend not putting the car seat in the front seat if you have a passenger-side air bag. If the bag inflates, it can knock the car seat around and injure baby.

MAKING HOME SAFE FOR BABY

It's important to make your house safe for your new baby. You may not think this is important when your baby is so small, but it is. There are many things you can do to protect your baby from the first day you bring her home.

You cannot babyproof your house, but you can make it safer. Accidents can and do (and will!) happen, so make your baby's environment as safe as you can make it. Keep in mind the following:

- Crib slats should be no farther than 2–3/8 inches (6cm) apart.
- Be sure the mattress fits securely.
- Keep the crib away from windows, wall decorations, heating units, climbable furniture, blind and drapery cords, and other possible dangers.
- Never use a pillow in a crib, your baby doesn't need one. It could also suffocate her.
- Keep the dropside up and locked when baby is in the crib.
- Keep mobiles and other crib toys out of baby's reach. You may have to remove them as baby grows older.

- Never hang a pacifier or any other object around baby's neck.
- Never leave a baby alone in the water, even if it's only a few inches deep. A baby can drown in as little as 1 inch of water.
- Never leave baby unattended on a sofa, chair, changing table or any other surface above the floor.
- Never put an infant seat on the counter or a table.
- Always use safety straps with baby equipment.
- Never hold or carry your baby while you're cooking, drinking a hot beverage or smoking a cigarette.
- If you warm formula or heat baby food in the microwave, shake the bottle or stir the food before serving to avoid any hot spots.
- Don't hang anything on stroller handles; the extra weight could cause the stroller to tip over.
- Always put your baby in a car seat. Be sure the car seat meets federal safety guidelines and is properly installed.
- Keep stairs and other areas well lit.
- Use nonslip mats in the tub and on the bathroom floor to help prevent falls.
- Install antiscald devices in tubs and showers.

8

Parenting Together

This is a remarkable time as you begin to share the joys and responsibilities of parenting with your partner. It may also be a time of wonder and concern for both of you as new parents. You may have many concerns. As a mother, you probably want to be the best mother ever. Your partner has many concerns of his own; he wants to be the best father he can be. And he may wonder what his role as a parent will be. You both may have many other questions, including those below.

- Will I be a good parent?
- Will my partner be a good parent?
- Will he or she support me and help me with the very important task of parenting?
- How will he or she help me with the baby?
- What can I do to help him or her be the best parent possible?

PRESERVING AND IMPROVING YOUR RELATIONSHIP WITH YOUR PARTNER

You have to work at a relationship to make it rewarding for both of you, especially now that there are more demands on your time and energy. These tips may help your relationship with your partner to grow stronger. Share them with him to help him preserve and improve your relationship as a couple. Your relationship involves *two* people!

- Take time to work at your relationship with your partner, even if you're both very busy.

- Be kind to each other. Compliment one another.

- When talking and interacting together, focus on what's important. Always show respect for the other person.

- Thank your partner for what he or she does for you.

- Set aside time each day for the two of you to be alone together. Give each other your undivided attention.

- Make an effort to remain close. Hug and kiss each other, even if you're not having sex.

- You may have to "create" time to be together. Let some things go. Cut corners in other tasks. Devise shortcuts.

- Go out alone together at least once every couple of weeks. Go to dinner or to the movies, or meet for lunch. Call each other on the phone to "connect" at least once a day.

- Leave messages for each other on the answering machine. Take the telephone off the hook some nights to give you private time together.

- Do tasks and chores together to cut the time you spend on them and to share an activity.

- Admit it's OK to have differences of opinion. Just be willing to try to understand how and why the other person thinks that way or wants to do something differently. Accept the fact that there are many "right" ways to get a job done.

In this chapter, we try to answer many questions, some you may not even know you have. Whether you find the specific answers you seek, it is our hope you will discover ways to help each other be good parents. Parenting may be the hardest job you will ever undertake, but it is also the most rewarding. Being able to help each other can make the job easier and more satisfying.

(**Authors' note:** In this chapter, we address information to both parents. In one section we may be talking to the new mom, in another, the new dad. In a few sections, we offer information for both parents. We will alert you to which parent the information is directed at the beginning of each section. You may find it helpful to read all the sections to understand better what your partner may be experiencing.)

S O S

 Involve your partner in your concerns. He may not know the answer, but you'll appreciate his help in figuring out what to do.

HELP YOUR PARTNER BEGIN TO PARENT

(For the New Mother)

Before a man becomes a father, much of whom he is is defined by his work. After his first child is born, that often changes—he is now a father—and that role becomes part of how he defines himself. Encourage and help your partner in his transition to fatherhood. One way your partner can become fully involved with his new baby is for you to help him prepare for the task.

You can begin this preparation before baby's birth. Childbirth classes and other prenatal preparation classes introduce dads-to-be to many aspects of childcare and parenting.

Encourage your partner to take time off after your baby's birth. He may have to arrange this leave of absence ahead of time, so plan for it before the baby is born. See the discussion of paternity leave that begins on page 150. It's great if your partner can stay home for a full week after the baby is born, but in many cases this may not be possible. As a new father, he may be able to make arrangements to spend more time with you and your baby. It allows him time to get to know his baby and to feel comfortable in his new role as a parent.

Even if you are breastfeeding, try to share feeding responsibilities. Expressing your milk for your partner to feed the baby can help them draw closer together; it can also provide a respite for you. If your partner wants to give the baby a bottle of expressed breast milk during the night, it allows you a longer period of uninterrupted sleep. You might really enjoy (and need) the sleep in the first few weeks of motherhood.

Divide tasks in the most logical way you can. If you need to rest before you start dinner, maybe dad can tend baby for an hour to give you a break. Then you can prepare dinner when you have more energy.

Trust your partner in his ability to care for your baby. Allow him the opportunity to be a good parent. Don't stand over him and correct him as he does everything. He'll probably make some mistakes, but babies are pretty resilient. Your baby may be able to handle mistakes more easily than you can. Giving your partner the space to develop his own parenting style helps him become more confident as a parent.

FAST FACTS

When a man helps care for his baby from birth, studies show he will continue to be involved in parenting as the child grows up.

BONDING WITH BABY

(For the New Father)

Women may have an advantage when it comes to bonding: Carrying the baby for 9 months helps a woman feel close to her baby even before it is born. Some experts feel bonding for the new father can also start before delivery. The father-to-be can feel the baby move inside the uterus by placing his hands on the mother-to-be's tummy.

It's important for a mother and baby to bond; it is equally important for a man to bond with his child. Bonding allows you to connect physically and emotionally with your baby. It doesn't happen instantly, and it isn't a one-time event. But it is one of the most important things you can do with your baby. It helps you feel your baby is your own.

You can bond with your baby by holding him close, gazing into his eyes and cooing at him. Stroking and rubbing the baby while making eye contact heightens the bonding effect. Babies readily respond to the human voice. Talking and singing help strengthen his connection to you. Don't worry if you can't carry a tune. Your baby will love to hear your voice.

It's important for you to spend time alone with your baby soon after birth. This time together strengthens your feelings of attachment. Take baby with you on errands, or just have baby close as you go through your day. You can carry him in a baby snuggler that you wear on your chest. Just hearing your voice, smelling your individual scent and being close to you will help both of you become closer to one another.

Don't be afraid to ask for help and guidance if you need it. No one is an expert immediately—not even your partner! It doesn't diminish you in any way to ask others for guidance. As a matter of fact, they will admire you for having the courage to know you need assistance and that you are confident enough to ask for it.

Talk to other parents, especially other fathers, about your concerns. Many men have had the same experiences and have experienced the same feelings of doubt. Their solutions to some of the problems you may have can save you worry and hassles. Your increased feelings of confidence help strengthen your bond with your new baby.

Some techniques fathers have used to bond with their baby include the following activities. Try them as you begin to build your relationship with your child.

- Lie on your side on the bed. Lay baby on his side facing you. Pull him close so he can feel your breath on his face. Sing or talk to him as you rub or stroke his body.
- Hold your baby so his head snuggles under your chin. (Be sure you have shaved recently so you don't give him whisker burn!) Sway from side to side, and coo or sing to him. He will feel your warm breath as you exhale.
- Lay baby on his stomach along your forearm. Support his head and chin with your hand. Let his legs hang down on either side of your arm. Carry him in this position, or sit in a chair together. Protect his head if you move around carrying him like this.
- Lie on the bed with your baby. Have your shirt off, and lay

your naked (or diapered) baby against your bare skin. (This position is also recommended for moms to promote bonding as soon baby is born.) Turn your baby's head to the side so he can hear your heartbeat. Relax together, and enjoy the closeness.

YOUR CHANGING RELATIONSHIP

(For the New Mother)

Your partner may feel his relationship with you is changing greatly. He may begin to look at you as the mother of his child, which can be a huge change in his thinking. Sometimes a man feels unnerved because he feels greater responsibility—for you and for the baby.

Your partner may also be experiencing other new emotions. He may feel left out because the bond between mother and child is so strong. He may feel ignored because his partner is now so involved with the new baby. He may hesitate to interact fully with his child because he doesn't feel confident that he can do it well. Or he may feel fearful that he won't be able to measure up to the responsibilities he now faces.

These, and many other feelings, are natural. It's important for you both to deal effectively with your feelings. The three "Cs" are important in this process—*communication, compromise* and *cooperation*. It may be hard to start a dialogue, but you can begin by sharing your own feelings about the situation. By being specific about what you're feeling, you'll encourage your partner to be specific about his concerns. Open communication can help you both. Discuss issues as they arise so you can deal with them. Be honest about your feelings and concerns.

There are other ways to help your partner in his transition to fatherhood after the baby arrives. Educate him about childcare;

you can learn together. Share books and articles about the many aspects of parenthood that you both may have questions about.

Help the new dad become an expert at some aspect of baby care. The more a person feels in control of a situation, the more he or she is willing to participate in it. For example, let your partner bathe baby when possible. Let him develop his own routine and control it. He may not do it like you would, but as long as the baby is clean (and of course, safe), what does it matter if he doesn't do it your way?

Be positive and encouraging. Your partner needs to know he's doing a good job and his efforts are appreciated. When he makes a mistake, accept it, provide as little correction as possible, praise what he has accomplished and move on.

Make things as easy as possible for your partner when he begins a new task or chore. As he becomes more adept at it, he can work out the details for himself. If he has your help from the beginning, he'll be more willing to pursue an activity than if he is just thrown into the task with little or no preparation.

HOW TO KEEP THE CLOSENESS IN YOUR RELATIONSHIP

(For Both the New Mother and the New Father)

With a new baby in the house, time tends to be a precious commodity; sometimes kindness, respect and thoughtfulness go out the window. It's important to work at the relationship you have with your partner. You're both in this parenthood thing together, and it's more rewarding for you both if you can grow closer with the added responsibilities instead of letting them separate you. There are many ways you can go about being kind to one another. Practice them together, and you may be surprised how strong your relationship becomes.

A stronger relationship between you provides security for your child.

Always be respectful to each other. No matter how tired you get or how frustrated you feel, maintaining respect for each other helps any situation. Censor words that can hurt one another; speak as you would to a friend. Be nice in your interactions; kindness goes a long way.

SOS

Talk to your doctor if sexual relations are extremely uncomfortable for you. He or she may have some suggestions on how to make the experience more enjoyable for you and your partner.

Focus on what is important, and ignore extraneous elements. If you want to discuss a particular problem, don't go into detail about problems you are having in other areas. Save that discussion for a time when you can sit down and talk in a relaxed way.

Compliment each other, whether it's about how your partner looks or about the fine job he or she is doing as a new parent. Everyone wants and needs to feel appreciated and loved, so remind each other again and again. Thank your partner for what he or she does for you. "Thank you" is very powerful and affirming in any relationship. It also shows respect for what the other person is doing (or attempting to do).

Make time to hug and to kiss each other. This nonsexual touching is important in a relationship, especially when you may not have time for sex. Set aside time every day for each other. Even if it's only 5 minutes at bedtime, knowing your partner is there for you (or you for him or her) with undivided attention

can be very strengthening in a relationship. It stresses the importance of the bond between the two of you and maintains commitment and communication.

Get out together when you can. Try to arrange a time away from home and baby that allows the two of you to focus only on each other. It doesn't have to be a long time—a half-hour walk in the early evening while a neighbor watches the baby can help you reconnect after days of hurry and rushing in your new life as a family. Or go for a walk with baby.

Laugh together. Life is serious but not all the time. Laughter heals, and it relieves tension. By laughing about various situations, you defuse them and relieve your tension. It's better to laugh than to cry, and it'll bring you closer together.

Listen, with respect, when your partner wants to talk. It's important to listen attentively to each other's concerns because it helps you stay connected. If you don't have time right then to talk, ask your partner to wait until you have the time to listen. Try to set a definite time to sit down to talk.

Admit that it's OK to have differences of opinion. Moms don't have all the answers; neither do dads. One of you may know more than the other, but that doesn't mean the other parent doesn't have valid points to make. It's often acceptable to do a chore or task in more than one way. You both could be right, so it's important to discuss a situation and come to an agreement. You might agree that you will each do the same task in different ways—that you'll each do it *your* way.

You can stay close in your relationship, even if you are both busy and stressed. It takes work, but it will pay off in many ways as you work together parenting your child.

WORKING TOGETHER AS PARENTS

(For Both the New Mother and the New Father)

You'll probably find that if you begin your role as parents by working together, you'll accomplish a great deal more. Agree in the beginning that it's OK for each of you to have different ways of doing things, but that you will be consistent in whatever you do.

Consistency is one of the most important aspects of raising a child. A child needs to know what the rules are and to have them enforced consistently. It's very confusing when the same action brings different reactions from the two parents. If you set limits, stand by them all the time. It's harder to do, but your child will be much happier and more well adjusted if you are consistent in your expectations, discipline and encouragement.

If you and your partner divide parenting duties and responsibilities as evenly as possible between the two of you, it will be easier for you to parent your baby. The fact that there are two of you will naturally introduce differences on the way some tasks should be handled, but this can be beneficial. Make an attempt to work together—not at odds with each other—to provide consistency in your child's life.

It's tough being a parent—it takes a lot of hard work and it can be very stressful. But rewards are great. Working together to create a team with your partner can increase those rewards.

One of the most common areas of concern is disagreements—it will be impossible for you and your partner to agree on everything. It may help to understand that each of you brings to this parenting relationship your own unique background of feelings and thoughts. You each may have a different "take" on a situation. This can create problems if you don't set up ways in advance to deal with the differences. The discussions below may provide with you some ways to deal with your particular situation.

Make plans *before* baby arrives. Sit down and discuss what your expectations are before your baby's birth. It's easier to find out what your partner believes about parenting before you each get caught up in the stress of parenting. You may be surprised (pleasantly or not) at what your partner believes his or her parental role will be.

Make an effort to share duties. It's a good idea for each of you to know how to care for your child completely, not just to know how to perform certain tasks. Because of illness or a change in the family situation, roles may change. If you are both experienced in all facets of caring for your baby, you'll be able to handle change more easily.

Agree what behaviors will not be tolerated. Establishing limits before a problem occurs provides direction for dealing with the problem when it arises.

Decide on a course of action to deal with a situation. Making decisions together helps to resolve a problem because you can be working toward the same goal and following the same plan. If discipline is necessary as the child grows older, both parents know what is appropriate.

Stay flexible. Different people have different ways of doing things that bring the same results. There is usually a variety of solutions at hand—be open to doing things a different way. It may save time and effort on your part to accept the "different" way your partner does something.

Support each other, even if you have a difference of opinion. Wait until you are alone to talk about your different takes on the situation and to work to resolve it. Remain united in front of your child.

Work toward an emotional balance. Support each other in your efforts to be good parents.

Consider each other's perspective. When a situation arises that you disagree on, try to see it from the other's point of view. Sometimes this shift in perspective can be very beneficial to you both.

··

FAST FACTS

After a baby is born, a couple's sex drive can be affected by stress, emotions and fatigue. Physical changes in the woman can also have an effect. Just relax and take it easy. It'll all come back to you in a little while!

··

MAKE TIME FOR EACH OTHER

(For Both the New Mother and the New Father)

With a new baby in the house, you may find you just don't seem to have time for each other like you did in the past. Sex may seem like a thing of the past. Sitting down and relating to one another as adults may seem like a luxury you can't indulge in any more. You used to spend time alone together, but you don't now.

Your relationship as a couple is still very important. In fact, it is more important than ever because you *need* your partner's love and support now more than ever before. Take heart. There are some things you can do for your partner and your relationship. It takes planning, work and time, but you'll be glad you did it when you reconnect.

- Make the minutes you have together count. All it takes is a little extra planning.
- Write notes to remind you to make the time you need to be together, even when you get caught up in the hectic business of taking care of baby.
- Exchange babysitting duties with another couple who has a new baby. You don't have to go out to a fancy restaurant or spend a lot of money. Just getting away and being together is what counts.
- Make a "date" for home. Set aside time to be together, just the two of you. After you put baby down, concentrate on each other. Watch a video together, play cards or drink a glass of wine.
- Cut corners when and where you can. Let the laundry go for a while. Leave cleaning up the kitchen until later. Devise shortcuts for doing chores and tasks.
- Instead of doing tasks separately, do them together. Work on a project with your partner, like planting the garden or washing the car. Doing something together gets the job done in half the time, and you can be with one another while you're doing it.
- You don't have to be perfect. If your house isn't spotless, it's OK. Wouldn't you rather have a little dust on the tables and a more solid relationship with your partner?

- Create time to be together. Get up a little earlier to share time. Call one another during the day to reconnect. Let unimportant things slide a little, such as returning phone calls to your friends, so you can be together.

PATERNITY LEAVE

(For the New Father)

Many men want to take time off from work after their child is born to get to know their baby better. They want to grow closer to their child, gain confidence in their parenting skills and become more comfortable as a parent. They also want to share this important time with their partner and help out around the house as she begins to recover.

Federal law guarantees a new father time to be at home with his baby, but few fathers take advantage of it. Many do not know much about the law. Others fear they might lose their job or be punished in some way if they request it. Below is information about paternity leave to help you decide if it's for you.

The Family and Medical Leave Act of 1993 (FMLA) grants workers (men and women) in companies with 50 or more employees up to 12 weeks of unpaid time off in the first year after a baby's birth. This act made millions of fathers eligible for paternity leave, but few have taken advantage of it.

....

FAST FACTS

The FMLA made millions of new fathers eligible for paternity leave, but fewer than 20% have taken time off under the provisions of the act.

....

Why haven't more men taken paternity leave? Most claim they can't afford to be without a paycheck. Others are afraid their bosses will think they aren't committed to their careers. Some fear they'll be fired from their jobs for taking the time off, although the law guarantees protection against this occurrence.

It's important for you to know you *can* take unpaid leave after your baby's birth. Being able to stay at home with your child is a wonderful gift. As one father who stayed at home for 6 weeks with his new son said, "You can't believe how quickly they grow and change. The time with him made me realize I could do the job (of parenting) and do it well. I think we'll always be close because of the time we shared together. I wouldn't give this up for the world!"

9

Returning to Work

Your pregnancy is over, and it seems as if most of the hard work is done. Yet you must still deal with child-care arrangements if you choose to return to work. You'll soon realize that balancing a family and a career requires organization and flexibility.

Whether to continue working outside the home after the baby's birth is one decision that many mothers wish they didn't have to make. However, due to financial necessity, staying home is not an option for many women.

In the 1950s and early 1960s, few women with children under the age of 6 worked outside the home. Today, a woman's salary may not be expendable. Returning to work after having a baby is as common as staying home.

THE COST OF WORKING:
IS IT WORTH IT?

Add up the following to find your total "working cost":

- cost of childcare
- cost of formula, if you will not continue breastfeeding when you return to work
- cost of duplicate equipment between home and childcare
- increase in taxes due to second income
- cost of travel to and from work
- cost of meals eaten out
- cost of extras, such as dry cleaning, clothing, other things you need if you work
- cost of any "treats" you reward yourself with, such as eating out, buying convenience foods, having someone clean the house for you

Follow steps 1–3 to determine what you are really earning. The bottom-line figure could surprise you.

1. Add together your take-home pay and benefits.

2. Deduct total working costs that you determined from the list above.

3. Divide this number by the total number of hours you spend away from home. This gives you a figure that represents how much you are making for each hour you are away from home and baby.

FAST FACTS

About 60% of all mothers work outside the home. Returning to work is more common than staying home.

IF YOU DECIDE TO STAY AT HOME

You may decide to stay home with your baby. If you do, the change from going out each day to work to staying at home can be traumatic. You may find staying at home isn't as easy as you thought it would be. It's true you won't have to worry about going to work or coming home to fix meals and do housework, but you may find staying home means less companionship, less money and the loss of your daily work routine.

If you have worked full time, you may not have met many people in your area. It's hard to make friends in your own neighborhood when you work all day. You may find your community soon becomes a substitute for your workplace. Don't bury yourself in motherhood and exclude all other activities. Make an effort to get out, meet people and get involved in new experiences with your baby.

FAST FACTS

Studies have shown that some women who left jobs to stay at home with baby were more distressed than new mothers who returned to work. Staying home may not be as easy as you think!

Stay in touch with your colleagues at work. Drop in to see them, or go out to lunch with a group. Call them, and stay on top of what is happening in your field.

BEFORE YOU RETURN TO WORK

If you decide to return to work, there are some things you can do to make the transition from home to career easier and more successful. Use what works for you in your particular situation.

....

FAST FACTS

When you plan to return to work, begin your work routine 1 week before you go back to establish your schedule. Get up at the time you normally would, feed your baby, make and eat your own breakfast, fix your lunch, pack your briefcase and pack baby's diaper bag. You may be surprised how long it takes to accomplish all these tasks.

....

2 Weeks Before You Return to Work

Experiment with various feeding techniques before you make any final decisions. You may decide to continue breastfeeding your baby. You can do this fairly easily if you are close to work or your job offers daycare services, allowing you to visit your baby when it's time to feed her. If these are not options, you will have to pump your breasts; using a dual-action pump gets the job done twice as fast. If you decide to switch to formula, eliminate one nursing every couple of days, beginning with the early-evening feeding. Switch to formula for day feedings. Eliminate the first and last feedings of the day as your final switch to formula.

Examine your wardrobe, and try clothes on! You may be larger in size (it's natural), or your body shape may have changed somewhat, making some clothes fit differently. Be sure you also try on shoes. If you intend to breastfeed or pump your breasts during working hours, you may need clothes that allow you to do this easily.

Finalize daycare arrangements. Visit the place you have planned to leave your child to check it out again and to make sure they have enrolled your child. It's also a good idea to have "sick-baby" arrangements in case your child gets sick and you can't take her to daycare. If you use a babysitter, you may need an alternate sitter in case your sitter gets sick.

Evaluate your needs at home. Will you be able to eliminate certain chores or adapt yourself to accepting different standards? You may not realize how valuable your time will be when you're at home—you probably won't want to spend your time keeping everything sparkling. Can you do chores more efficiently, such as cooking ahead for the week or shopping only once a week? Can you hire someone to do some cleaning for you?

1 Week Before You Return to Work

Begin your work routine this week. Get up at the time you normally rise when you are going to work. Feed your baby on the new schedule. Make and eat your own breakfast. Allow time to pack a lunch and fill baby's diaper bag.

Make a list of all the supplies. You will need a lot of things for baby at home and at daycare. Consider diapers, formula, baby clothes, extra bottles, a second car seat and anything else you may need for your baby's care and comfort.

Choose your clothes. Lay clothes out the night before you go back to work. Be sure everything is OK to wear. If you continue to breastfeed, have a couple of clothing changes available at your office, and have a good supply of breast pads. Pack your diaper bag with baby's things to take to daycare. Eat a good meal, and go to bed early to get a good night's sleep.

FAST FACTS

Try on shoes you may not have worn for a while. Your shoe size may increase 1/2 to 1 full size during pregnancy. Often this increase is permanent, and your feet will remain larger, even after baby's birth.

The Day You Return to Work

If possible, choose a Thursday to return to work. It helps you get into the routine of working, but you'll only work a short week. This plan allows you to replenish your energy for the following 5-day work week. If you can start back with fewer hours, that also helps. Five hours a day for a week is a good plan, gradually increasing to 8 hours a day.

Plan easy-to-fix meals for the first few weeks after you start working. Or prepare and freeze some dishes so you don't have to cook. You might even want to get take-home food a couple of times.

Don't get upset if you feel a great loss when you return to work. It's OK to grieve and to feel some guilt when you leave your baby. You may even feel some relief to get back to work. That's OK, too.

When you return to work, some co-workers will be very supportive; others may be insensitive to how you are feeling. It's important to find ways to ease the transition from being at home to going back to work.

You may encounter some of your greatest challenges when you return home *after* work. You may be tired and hungry, but you probably won't be able to sit down and rest because your family will need your time and attention. You may need to arrange with your partner to share many new "baby" responsibilities.

Give your baby your total attention when you are with her. Have your partner try to do the same by having him spend some quality time with her. Also set aside some time for just you and your partner. You'll probably both need it after a full day. It's important to manage your time; you'll have many new demands on you and your resources.

Try to make a plan, and stick to it. You can't do everything, so don't try. Delegate some responsibilities to others. Do what you can, and let less important things go. You may not be able to do as much as you could before your baby was born, so you may need to change your expectations.

CHILDCARE DECISIONS

Arranging childcare can be a daunting task. There are many decisions you must make in selecting someone to care for your baby. Of course, you want to pick the best environment and caregiver for your child. The best way to do that is to know what your options are before you begin.

There are many choices when it comes to childcare. Any situation could be right for you, but you must first examine your needs and the needs of your child before you can decide which one to pursue. Below is a discussion of various types of childcare situations. Your options for childcare include in-your-home care by a family relative, in-your-home care by a nonrelative, care in a caregiver's home and a childcare center

In-Home Care

You may decide on in-home care, either by a relative or nonrelative. Having someone come to your home to take care of your child is usually very easy. You don't have to get the baby ready before you go in the morning, and you never have to take your child out in bad weather. It also takes less time in the morning and evening if you don't have to drop off or to pick up your baby.

In-home care is an excellent choice for a baby or small child because it provides one-to-one attention if you only have one child at home. The environment is also familiar to the child.

When the caregiver is a relative, such as a grandparent, an aunt or someone else in the family, you may find it more challenging than you anticipated. It may be more difficult to maintain your relationship with your caregiver while asking or telling him or her to do things the way you want them done.

When the caregiver is a nonrelative, you may find it very expensive to have this person come to your home. You are also hiring someone you do not know to come into your home and tend your child. You must be diligent in asking for references and checking them out thoroughly.

One drawback to having in-home care is the isolation your child may feel as she grows older. Children need to interact with other children so they can learn to share and to play together.

While in-home care can be an excellent choice for your baby, as she gets older you may have to make special arrangements to create opportunities for your child to be with other children.

Care in a Caregiver's Home

Taking your child to someone else's home is an option that many parents choose. Often these homes have small group sizes that offer more flexibility for parents, such as keeping the child longer on a day when you have a late meeting you cannot avoid. A homelike setting will make your child feel comfortable, and she may receive lots of attention. In addition, she may get plenty of interaction with peers if the home also cares for other children.

However, home daycare situations are not regulated in every state, so you must check out each situation very carefully. Contact your state's Department of Social Services, and ask about legal requirements. In some places, local agencies oversee caregivers who are members of their organization. Those who provide care must abide by certain standards, such as the maximum number of children allowed in the home (including their own) and the maximum fees they may charge. They must also be certified in CPR and first-aid.

Steps for Finding an In-Home Caregiver

Whether you choose to have someone come to your home or to take your child to another person's home, there are some steps you can follow to find a care provider.

Advertise. Put ads in local newspapers and church bulletins to find someone to interview. State how many children are to be cared for and their ages. Include information on the days and hours care is needed, the amount or type of experience you require and any other particulars. State that references will be required, and they will be checked.

Conduct telephone interviews. You may have to interview a lot of caregivers before you find one you feel comfortable with. Talk to candidates on the telephone first to determine whether you want to interview them. Ask about their experience, qualifications, childcare philosophy and what they are seeking in a position. Then decide if you want to pursue the contact with an interview in person.

Make a list. Note your concerns, including the days and hours someone is needed, the duties to be performed, the need for a driver's license and what kind of benefits policy will be supplied. Discuss these things with the potential caregiver.

Check all references. Have the potential caregiver provide you with the names and phone numbers of people he or she has worked for in the past. Call each of the families, let them know you are considering this person as a caregiver and discuss it with them.

Investigate the situation. After you hire someone, monitor the situation occasionally by dropping by unannounced. See how everything is being managed when you do. Pay attention to how your child reacts each time you leave or arrive; although some separation anxiety is normal at times, your child's reactions can give you a clue as to how she feels about the caregiver.

Responsibilities to Your Caregiver

Your caregiver has certain responsibilities to you, and you have responsibilities to him or her. Be on time when you drop your child off or pick her up. Call if you're going to be late, even if the care is in your own home. Pay the caregiver when fees are due. Provide diapers, formula or expressed breast milk, extra clothes and personal items for the baby when necessary.

You must pay federal, state and local taxes for your care provider, including Social Security and Medicare taxes. If the person works in your home, you may also need to pay Workers' Compensation and unemployment insurance taxes. Contact the Internal Revenue Service and your state's Department of Economic Security for further information.

Childcare Centers

A childcare center is an environment in which many children are cared for in a larger setting. Centers vary widely in the facilities and activities they provide, the amount of attention they give each child, group sizes and childcare philosophy.

Inquire about the training required for each childcare provider or teacher. Some facilities expect more from a care provider than others. In some cases, a facility hires only trained, qualified personnel; in other cases, the facility provides training.

You may find some childcare centers do not accept infants. Often centers focus more on older children because infants take a great deal of time and attention. If the center accepts infants, the ratio of caregivers to children should be about one adult to every three or four children (up to age 2). For older children, one adult for every four to six 2-year-olds and one adult for every seven to eight 3-year-olds is considered the maximum.

You want the facility you choose to offer quality childcare, but don't be fooled by a state-of-the-art center. The cleanest, brightest place is useless without the right kind of caregivers. Check out the center thoroughly; visit it by appointment, then stop in unannounced a few times. Meet the person in charge and the people who will care for your child. Ask for references from parents whose children are currently being cared for there. Call and talk to parents before making a final decision.

Caring for an Infant

Babies have special needs that a preschool cannot meet. Be sure the place you choose for your infant can meet those needs. A baby must be changed and fed, but she also has other needs. A baby needs to be held and interacted with; she needs to be comforted when she is afraid. She needs to rest at certain times each day.

When searching for a place, keep your baby's needs in mind. Evaluate every situation according to whether it meets those needs.

Finding Childcare for Your Child

You might find it difficult to begin your search for someone to care for your child. Where do you start? There are many things you can do in your quest to find the best care situation for your child, and there are many ways to find out about childcare. Use the following suggestions to help you find someone to care for your baby.

- Ask friends, family and co-workers for referrals to people or places they know about. Talk to people in your area. Ask at your church about any programs they may sponsor.

- Call a local referral agency, or contact Child Care Aware at 1-800-424-2246 for a local childcare resource.
- If you're interested in hiring a nanny to provide care in your home, contact a referral agency; they are usually listed in the yellow pages.

Whomever you choose to provide care for your child, *be sure* to check their references carefully before you make a final decision. This applies to centers as well as in-home caregivers (your home or theirs).

The Cost of Childcare

Paying for childcare can be a big-budget item in your household expenses. For some families, it can cost 25% or more of their household budget. The cost of infant and toddler care (through age 3) is the highest—it can range from $100 to $200 (or more) a week, depending on where you live and the type of care you choose. In-home care can be more costly, with placement fees and additional fees you negotiate based on extra tasks you want the caregiver to perform.

Public funding is available for some limited-income families. Title EE is a program paid for with federal funds. Call your local Department of Social Services to find out if you are eligible.

Other programs to help deal with childcare costs include a federal tax-credit program, the dependent-care assistance program and earned-income tax credit. These three programs are regulated by the federal government; contact the Internal Revenue service at 1-800-829-1040 for further information.

When to Start Looking for Childcare

Finding the best situation for your baby can take time. Start the process several weeks (maybe several months, particularly in special situations like twins) before you need it. Often this means finding childcare *before* your baby is born.

Some situations may require getting on a waiting list. There is a shortage of quality childcare for children under age 2. If you find a care provider you are comfortable with, but it's not time to leave your baby, ask if you can put down a deposit and set a date for childcare to begin. Keep in touch with the care provider, and plan to meet before you place your child in daily care.

Special-Care Needs

In some situations, your child may have special-care needs. If your baby is born with a disability or a health problem that needs one-on-one attention, you may have a harder time finding appropriately qualified childcare. In these special cases, you may have to spend extra time to find the right situation to meet your child's needs.

Contact the hospital where your child has been cared for and ask for references, or contact your pediatrician. They may be in contact with someone who can help you. If your child has special needs, it may be better to arrange for a care provider to come to your home.

Caring for a Sick Child

All children come down with colds, the flu or diarrhea at some time. Today, there are ways to deal with your child's illness if you can't take time off from work to stay at home with her. In many places, "sick-child" daycare centers are available. They are usually attached to a regular daycare facility, although some are connected with hospitals. A sick-child center provides a comfortable place where a child who is ill can rest or participate in quiet activities, such as story time.

This kind of facility is often headed by a registered nurse who can administer medication when necessary. Fees for this type of service run from $25 to $55 a day.

Some cities have "on-call" in-home care providers who come to your home when your child is too sick to be taken anywhere. The program is usually run by an agency that deals with child-care, and these caregivers normally charge by the hour. You may have to wait a day or so for a provider, but this service can be an excellent way to care for a child who is too ill to be taken away from home.

S O S

When you return to work, ask for a change in hours or a change in your work load if you feel it would help you ease back into your job.

CAN YOU MODIFY YOUR WORK SITUATION?

With careful exploration, you may find ways to modify your current work situation so everyone is happy—you, your boss, your partner and your baby. Examine various work schedules to determine what may suit your needs.

Some women decide to keep working but not full time. If there is some way you can cut your hours and work part time, you may be happier. It may mean less money, but your peace of mind may compensate for the monetary loss. Ask your employer if you can cut your hours or share a job with someone else. There may be another person who does the same type of job as you do in the company who would also like to work only part time.

Find out if flex-time programs are available at your company. In some cases, you can modify your work schedule; for example, you could work four 10-hour days. In other cases, you may be able to come in early and leave early, or arrive late and leave late. You may be able to set your own schedule, as long as you get your work done.

If you work part time or flex time, childcare may be harder to find. Some centers are more flexible than others, and some in-home care providers (their home or yours) welcome the break. In other cases, you may find less flexibility with a center—you usually pay on a weekly basis, whether your child is there or not. If an in-home care provider depends on the income from tending your child, a lighter schedule means less money.

A third solution might be to work at home part time or full time. Many companies are now set up to allow workers (men and women) to work at home. With planning and foresight, working from home can be a positive experience for you and your baby.

BREASTFEEDING AND WORK

Breastfeeding is important to many women, and they don't want to have to stop when they return to work. It's possible to breast-feed your baby even after you return to work. If you breastfeed exclusively, you will have to pump your breasts or arrange to see your baby during the day. Or you can nurse your baby at home and feed expressed breast milk or formula when you're away. It takes a little more time, but if it's important to you, do it. (See Chapter 4 for an in-depth discussion of breastfeeding.)

SOS

Let your supervisor know if you are breastfeeding or need to empty your breasts during the day. You can become very uncomfortable if you can't express your milk by either feeding your baby or using a breast pump.

One way to smooth the back-to-work transition for you and baby is to begin storing breast milk for a couple of weeks before you return to work. Use an electric breast pump to express milk between feedings about 2 weeks before you start work. Don't start expressing milk sooner because you may produce too much milk. A breast pump that has a double-pumping feature empties both breasts at once. Freeze expressed milk in quantities from 1 ounce to 4 ounces. This provides your caregiver with options as to how much to thaw for a particular feeding.

It may be possible to pump then store breast milk while you're at work. You may be very uncomfortable if you don't pump your breasts because your milk continues to flow in. Take a breast pump with you, and refrigerate or discard breast milk after it is pumped.

If you remain at home until your baby is between 4 and 6 months old, your baby may be able to skip the bottle and start drinking from a cup. Earlier than 4 months, she will need to learn to drink from a bottle. After 4 weeks of nursing exclusively, your baby will be ready to try a bottle without compromising your milk supply or her nursing technique. With the first bottle feedings, let someone else feed the baby the bottle when she's not too hungry. Bottlefeed her around the same time she will receive a bottle once you return to work.

10

Planning and Preparing for Your Next Pregnancy

It may seem strange to discuss your next pregnancy when you've just had a baby, but it's an important consideration. Most women want to wait for a while after they have a baby before even thinking about pregnancy again. Some women want to get pregnant again very quickly. Other women are surprised when they find themselves pregnant again because they didn't think about birth control. Below is a discussion of many aspects of this issue that you may not have thought about.

ASK YOUR DOCTOR QUESTIONS

Your 6-week postpartum checkup is a good time to ask questions about future pregnancies. Discuss concerns about your re-

cent delivery and about any complications you had. This information can be helpful to you with your next pregnancy, especially if you move or deliver with a different doctor or hospital. Some common questions include those listed below.

- Are there things I need to do before getting pregnant again, such as having medical tests or vaccinations?
- Are there any warning signs I need to watch for during subsequent pregnancies?
- Were there complications during my last pregnancy that may recur, such as gestational diabetes?
- Will I need to have a C-section again next time or could I safely try labor?

Women frequently ask, "How long should I wait before getting pregnant again?" You should recover physically and emotionally before attempting pregnancy again, regardless of the type of delivery (C-section or vaginal delivery). How long your recovery takes is influenced by several factors, including the following:

- complications during your previous pregnancy, such as high blood pressure or gestational diabetes
- the length or difficulty of labor and delivery
- problems with bleeding or infection
- chronic medical problems, such as diabetes
- how much help you get at home from friends or family
- what responsibilities you already have at home (how many children and what are their ages?)

When we speak of *physical recovery*, we mean you are able to do all the normal activities that you did before your pregnancy, you are exercising regularly, your weight is where you want it to be and there are no medical or physical problems requiring tests or treatments that should be checked out before getting pregnant. For most women, this is at least 6 months to a year after delivery, at the earliest. These guidelines are for recovery after either a vaginal or a Cesarean delivery. Recovery from a C-section usually takes longer than a vaginal delivery.

DISCONTINUING CONTRACEPTION BEFORE YOUR NEXT PREGNANCY

If you are using one of the doctor-prescribed methods of birth control, talk to your physician about when to stop using it for your next pregnancy. In many cases, your doctor will want you to stop using the method or to have it removed, such as with an IUD or Norplant, then wait for a certain number of regular menstrual cycles to occur before attempting pregnancy. Waiting until your menstrual cycle becomes more regular helps predict more accurately a due date for your next pregnancy.

PREGNANCY WITHIN THE FIRST YEAR

Most doctors recommend you not get pregnant for at least 1 year after your delivery. During this time, you will be extremely busy with your baby and recovery from pregnancy, labor and delivery. It can be difficult to adjust to your new life and still find time for yourself and your partner.

If you had any problems or complications during or after your pregnancy, take care of them so if you do get pregnant again, you are in the best possible shape. If you take medication on a regular basis, talk with your doctor before stopping or changing it. Find out if medications you are taking can harm a fetus. Usually an attempt is made to decrease the amount of medication taken, if possible, and to avoid or to stop taking medications that you don't need or that may be harmful to you and your developing baby. Let your doctor help you with this.

Women often want to know if there is an exact time interval that is safe before trying to get pregnant. The answer is different for every woman. Getting pregnant right away can affect your ability to breastfeed. Most doctors recommend stopping breastfeeding if you are pregnant, which can shorten the time you can provide the benefits of breastfeeding to your baby.

In addition, whether you had an easy first pregnancy and delivery doesn't usually predict what will happen in subsequent pregnancies. Each pregnancy tends to be unique; don't count on future pregnancies being easy or hard, based on what has happened before.

A couple needs to recover physically and emotionally. Recovering physically may take 6 months, a year or even longer.

Part of this challenge is the full-time "job" required in caring for a newborn without a lot of time left for you. It can be done, though it may take trading childcare with a friend to get time for exercise or other personal time.

Many women are able to lose most, but not all, of the weight they gained during pregnancy. With each pregnancy they start out 5 to 10 pounds heavier than their previous pregnancy. During subsequent pregnancies, it can be even harder to control your weight; after two or three pregnancies, you may have gained 10 to 30 pounds that can be very hard to lose.

FAST FACTS

It takes your body nearly 1 full year to recover from a pregnancy.

DISCUSSING COMPLICATIONS

If you had complications during your pregnancy, discuss them with your doctor. Find out what to watch for as you recover and if any complications during this pregnancy could affect another pregnancy. This includes medications or medical tests needed. Most complications, such as anemia or gestational diabetes during pregnancy, begin to improve after delivery and nothing more will need to be done. Some problems, such as high blood pressure, need to be evaluated after you have delivered. Discuss any problems with your doctor before attempting pregnancy again.

If you had a C-section, it may be necessary to deliver by C-section again. Discuss this with your doctor. It may be possible to have labor after a previous C-section and to deliver vaginally. This is called *VBAC* (vaginal birth after C-section).

If you had gestational diabetes, ask whether it might be a problem next time. Now is a good time to ask about these things while they are fresh in your mind as well as in your doctor's mind. The answers to questions about this pregnancy could make a big difference in preparing for future pregnancies.

Consider all these things, and take whatever action is necessary before stopping contraception. (You may not think that you are trying to get pregnant, but if you are not using contraception, you are trying to get pregnant!) Today, it is more common to talk about the "12 months" of pregnancy, instead of 9 months, meaning you should begin taking care of yourself as though you are already pregnant 3 months *before* you get pregnant.

You may wish to read the other pregnancy books in this series, *Your Pregnancy Week by Week, Your Pregnancy Questions and Answers, Your Pregnancy—Every Woman's Guide* and *Your Pregnancy After 35*, for information on preparing for pregnancy. Reading them can be very helpful in preparing for pregnancy, even if you have been pregnant before.

Whether you decide to have another baby in a year or 2, or to wait longer, it's important to be prepared. By reading this book and following the suggestions for eating right and exercising, you can make your pregnancy recovery as complete as possible. By taking the best care of yourself, if you decide to become pregnant again, you'll go a long way in ensuring the good health of yourself and your next baby.

Index